The Poetry of Bret Harte

Francis Bret Harte was born on August 25, 1836 in Albany New York.

As a young boy Harte developed an early love of books and reading. He first published at the tender age of 11; a satirical poem titled "Autumn Musings." Expecting praise he encountered anything but and was later to write "Such a shock was their ridicule to me that I wonder that I ever wrote another line of verse."

By age 13 his formal education was at an end and four years later, in 1853, the family moved to California. Here the young man worked in a variety of capacities; miner, teacher, messenger, and journalist.

But it was also here on the West coast that he found the stories and inspiration for the works that would endure his fame across the literary world. He championed the early writings of Mark Twain. He was instrumental in propelling the short story genre forward and brought tales of the Old West and the Gold Rush to a greater audience. At the height of his fame we would entertain staggering monetary offers to write for monthly magazines.

His talents extended to poetry, plays, lectures, book reviews, editorials, and magazine sketches. As he moved location initially further east to New York and then through Consular appointments to Europe and finally to settle in England his audience diminished but he continued to experiment, to write and to publish.

Bret Harte died of throat cancer on May 5th 1902 and is buried in St Peter's Church in Frimley, Surrey, England.

Index Of Poems

I. NATIONAL

JOHN BURNS OF GETTYSBURG

Have you heard the story that gossips tell
Of Burns of Gettysburg? No? Ah, well:
Brief is the glory that hero earns,
Briefer the story of poor John Burns.
He was the fellow who won renown,
The only man who didn't back down
When the rebels rode through his native town;
But held his own in the fight next day,
When all his townsfolk ran away.
That was in July sixty-three,
The very day that General Lee,
Flower of Southern chivalry,
Baffled and beaten, backward reeled
From a stubborn Meade and a barren field.

I might tell how but the day before
John Burns stood at his cottage door,
Looking down the village street,
Where, in the shade of his peaceful vine,
He heard the low of his gathered kine,
And felt their breath with incense sweet;
Or I might say, when the sunset burned
The old farm gable, he thought it turned
The milk that fell like a babbling flood
Into the milk-pail red as blood!
Or how he fancied the hum of bees
Were bullets buzzing among the trees.
But all such fanciful thoughts as these
Were strange to a practical man like Burns,
Who minded only his own concerns,
Troubled no more by fancies fine
Than one of his calm-eyed, long-tailed kine,
Quite old-fashioned and matter-of-fact,

Slow to argue, but quick to act.
That was the reason, as some folk say,
He fought so well on that terrible day.

And it was terrible. On the right
Raged for hours the heady fight,
Thundered the battery's double bass,
Difficult music for men to face
While on the left, where now the graves
Undulate like the living waves
That all that day unceasing swept
Up to the pits the rebels kept
Round shot ploughed the upland glades,
Sown with bullets, reaped with blades;
Shattered fences here and there
Tossed their splinters in the air;
The very trees were stripped and bare;
The barns that once held yellow grain
Were heaped with harvests of the slain;
The cattle bellowed on the plain,
The turkeys screamed with might and main,
And brooding barn-fowl left their rest
With strange shells bursting in each nest.

Just where the tide of battle turns,
Erect and lonely stood old John Burns.
How do you think the man was dressed?
He wore an ancient long buff vest,
Yellow as saffron, but his best;
And buttoned over his manly breast
Was a bright blue coat, with a rolling collar,
And large gilt buttons, size of a dollar,
With tails that the country-folk called "swaller."
He wore a broad-brimmed, bell-crowned hat,
White as the locks on which it sat.
Never had such a sight been seen
For forty years on the village green,
Since old John Burns was a country beau,
And went to the "quiltings" long ago.

Close at his elbows all that day,
Veterans of the Peninsula,
Sunburnt and bearded, charged away;
And striplings, downy of lip and chin,
Clerks that the Home Guard mustered in,
Glanced, as they passed, at the hat he wore,
Then at the rifle his right hand bore,
And hailed him, from out their youthful lore,
With scraps of a slangy repertoire:
"How are you, White Hat?" "Put her through!"
"Your head's level!" and "Bully for you!"

Called him "Daddy," begged he'd disclose
The name of the tailor who made his clothes,
And what was the value he set on those;
While Burns, unmindful of jeer and scoff,
Stood there picking the rebels off,
With his long brown rifle and bell-crown hat,
And the swallow-tails they were laughing at.

'Twas but a moment, for that respect
Which clothes all courage their voices checked;
And something the wildest could understand
Spake in the old man's strong right hand,
And his corded throat, and the lurking frown
Of his eyebrows under his old bell-crown;
Until, as they gazed, there crept an awe
Through the ranks in whispers, and some men saw,
In the antique vestments and long white hair,
The Past of the Nation in battle there;
And some of the soldiers since declare
That the gleam of his old white hat afar,
Like the crested plume of the brave Navarre,
That day was their oriflamme of war.

So raged the battle. You know the rest:
How the rebels, beaten and backward pressed,
Broke at the final charge and ran.
At which John Burns, a practical man
Shouldered his rifle, unbent his brows,
And then went back to his bees and cows.

That is the story of old John Burns;
This is the moral the reader learns:
In fighting the battle, the question's whether
You'll show a hat that's white, or a feather!

"HOW ARE YOU, SANITARY?"

Down the picket-guarded lane
Rolled the comfort-laden wain,
Cheered by shouts that shook the plain,
    Soldier-like and merry:
Phrases such as camps may teach,
Sabre-cuts of Saxon speech,
Such as "Bully!" "Them's the peach!"
    "Wade in, Sanitary!"

Right and left the caissons drew
As the car went lumbering through,
Quick succeeding in review

Squadrons military;
Sunburnt men with beards like frieze,
Smooth-faced boys, and cries like these,
"U. S. San. Com." "That's the cheese!"
"Pass in, Sanitary!"

In such cheer it struggled on
Till the battle front was won:
Then the car, its journey done,
Lo! was stationary;
And where bullets whistling fly
Came the sadder, fainter cry,
"Help us, brothers, ere we die,
Save us, Sanitary!"

Such the work. The phantom flies,
Wrapped in battle clouds that rise:
But the brave, whose dying eyes,
Veiled and visionary,
See the jasper gates swung wide,
See the parted throng outside
Hears the voice to those who ride:
"Pass in, Sanitary!"

BATTLE BUNNY

(MALVERN HILL, 1864)

"After the men were ordered to lie down, a white rabbit, which had been hopping hither and thither over the field swept by grape and musketry, took refuge among the skirmishers, in the breast of a corporal." Report of the Battle of Malvern Hill.

Bunny, lying in the grass,
Saw the shining column pass;
Saw the starry banner fly,
Saw the chargers fret and fume,
Saw the flapping hat and plume,
Saw them with his moist and shy
Most unspeculative eye,
Thinking only, in the dew,
That it was a fine review.

Till a flash, not all of steel,
Where the rolling caissons wheel,
Brought a rumble and a roar
Rolling down that velvet floor,
And like blows of autumn flail
Sharply threshed the iron hail.

Bunny, thrilled by unknown fears,
Raised his soft and pointed ears,
Mumbled his prehensile lip,
Quivered his pulsating hip,
As the sharp vindictive yell
Rose above the screaming shell;
Thought the world and all its men,
All the charging squadrons meant,
All were rabbit-hunters then,
All to capture him intent.
Bunny was not much to blame:
Wiser folk have thought the same,
Wiser folk who think they spy
Every ill begins with "I."

Wildly panting here and there,
Bunny sought the freer air,
Till he hopped below the hill,
And saw, lying close and still,
Men with muskets in their hands.
(Never Bunny understands
That hypocrisy of sleep,
In the vigils grim they keep,
As recumbent on that spot
They elude the level shot.)

One, a grave and quiet man,
Thinking of his wife and child
Far beyond the Rapidan,
Where the Androscoggin smiled
Felt the little rabbit creep,
Nestling by his arm and side,
Wakened from strategic sleep,
To that soft appeal replied,
Drew him to his blackened breast,
And - But you have guessed the rest.

Softly o'er that chosen pair
Omnipresent Love and Care
Drew a mightier Hand and Arm,
Shielding them from every harm;
Right and left the bullets waved,
Saved the saviour for the saved.

Who believes that equal grace
God extends in every place,
Little difference he scans
Twixt a rabbit's God and man's.

THE REVEILLE

Hark! I hear the tramp of thousands,
And of armed men the hum;
Lo! a nation's hosts have gathered
Round the quick alarming drum,
Saying, "Come,
Freemen, come!
Ere your heritage be wasted," said the quick alarming drum.

"Let me of my heart take counsel:
War is not of life the sum;
Who shall stay and reap the harvest
When the autumn days shall come?"
But the drum
Echoed, "Come!
Death shall reap the braver harvest," said the solemn-sounding drum.

"But when won the coming battle,
What of profit springs therefrom?
What if conquest, subjugation,
Even greater ills become?"
But the drum
Answered, "Come!
You must do the sum to prove it," said the Yankee answering drum.

"What if, 'mid the cannons' thunder,
Whistling shot and bursting bomb,
When my brothers fall around me,
Should my heart grow cold and numb?"
But the drum
Answered, "Come!
Better there in death united, than in life a recreant. Come!"

Thus they answered, hoping, fearing,
Some in faith, and doubting some,
Till a trumpet-voice proclaiming,
Said, "My chosen people, come!"
Then the drum,
Lo! was dumb,
For the great heart of the nation, throbbing, answered, "Lord, we come!"

OUR PRIVILEGE

Not ours, where battle smoke upcurls,
And battle dews lie wet,
To meet the charge that treason hurls
By sword and bayonet.

Not ours to guide the fatal scythe
The fleshless Reaper wields;
The harvest moon looks calmly down
Upon our peaceful fields.

The long grass dimples on the hill,
The pines sing by the sea,
And Plenty, from her golden horn,
Is pouring far and free.

O brothers by the farther sea!
Think still our faith is warm;
The same bright flag above us waves
That swathed our baby form.

The same red blood that dyes your fields
Here throbs in patriot pride,
The blood that flowed when Lander fell,
And Baker's crimson tide.

And thus apart our hearts keep time
With every pulse ye feel,
And Mercy's ringing gold shall chime
With Valor's clashing steel.

RELIEVING GUARD

THOMAS STARR KING. OBIIT MARCH 4, 1864

Came the relief. "What, sentry, ho!
How passed the night through thy long waking?"
"Cold, cheerless, dark, as may befit
The hour before the dawn is breaking."

"No sight? no sound?" "No; nothing save
The plover from the marshes calling,
And in yon western sky, about
An hour ago, a star was falling."

"A star? There's nothing strange in that."
"No, nothing; but, above the thicket,
Somehow it seemed to me that God
Somewhere had just relieved a picket."

THE GODDESS

CONTRIBUTED TO THE FAIR FOR THE LADIES' PATRIOTIC FUND OF THE PACIFIC

"Who comes?" The sentry's warning cry
Rings sharply on the evening air:
Who comes? The challenge: no reply,
Yet something motions there.

A woman, by those graceful folds;
A soldier, by that martial tread:
"Advance three paces. Halt! until
Thy name and rank be said."

"My name? Her name, in ancient song,
Who fearless from Olympus came:
Look on me! Mortals know me best
In battle and in flame."

"Enough! I know that clarion voice;
I know that gleaming eye and helm,
Those crimson lips, and in their dew
The best blood of the realm.

"The young, the brave, the good and wise,
Have fallen in thy curst embrace:
The juices of the grapes of wrath
Still stain thy guilty face.

"My brother lies in yonder field,
Face downward to the quiet grass:
Go back! he cannot see thee now;
But here thou shalt not pass."

A crack upon the evening air,
A wakened echo from the hill:
The watchdog on the distant shore
Gives mouth, and all is still.

The sentry with his brother lies
Face downward on the quiet grass;
And by him, in the pale moonshine,
A shadow seems to pass.

No lance or warlike shield it bears:
A helmet in its pitying hands
Brings water from the nearest brook,
To meet his last demands.

Can this be she of haughty mien,
The goddess of the sword and shield?
Ah, yes! The Grecian poet's myth
Sways still each battlefield.

For not alone that rugged War
Some grace or charm from Beauty gains;
But, when the goddess' work is done,
The woman's still remains.

ON A PEN OF THOMAS STARR KING

This is the reed the dead musician dropped,
With tuneful magic in its sheath still hidden;
The prompt allegro of its music stopped,
Its melodies unbidden.

But who shall finish the unfinished strain,
Or wake the instrument to awe and wonder,
And bid the slender barrel breathe again,
An organ-pipe of thunder!

His pen! what humbler memories cling about
Its golden curves! what shapes and laughing graces
Slipped from its point, when his full heart went out
In smiles and courtly phrases?

The truth, half jesting, half in earnest flung;
The word of cheer, with recognition in it;
The note of alms, whose golden speech outrung
The golden gift within it.

But all in vain the enchanter's wand we wave:
No stroke of ours recalls his magic vision:
The incantation that its power gave
Sleeps with the dead magician.

A SECOND REVIEW OF THE GRAND ARMY

I read last night of the grand review
In Washington's chiefest avenue,
Two hundred thousand men in blue,
I think they said was the number,
Till I seemed to hear their trampling feet,
The bugle blast and the drum's quick beat,
The clatter of hoofs in the stony street,
The cheers of people who came to greet,
And the thousand details that to repeat
Would only my verse encumber,
Till I fell in a reverie, sad and sweet,
And then to a fitful slumber.

When, lo! in a vision I seemed to stand
In the lonely Capitol. On each hand
Far stretched the portico, dim and grand
Its columns ranged like a martial band
Of sheeted spectres, whom some command
Had called to a last reviewing.
And the streets of the city were white and bare,
No footfall echoed across the square;
But out of the misty midnight air
I heard in the distance a trumpet blare,
And the wandering night-winds seemed to bear
The sound of a far tattooing.

Then I held my breath with fear and dread
For into the square, with a brazen tread,
There rode a figure whose stately head
O'erlooked the review that morning,
That never bowed from its firm-set seat
When the living column passed its feet,
Yet now rode steadily up the street
To the phantom bugle's warning:

Till it reached the Capitol square, and wheeled,
And there in the moonlight stood revealed
A well-known form that in State and field
Had led our patriot sires:
Whose face was turned to the sleeping camp,
Afar through the river's fog and damp,
That showed no flicker, nor waning lamp,
Nor wasted bivouac fires.

And I saw a phantom army come,
With never a sound of fife or drum,
But keeping time to a throbbing hum
Of wailing and lamentation:
The martyred heroes of Malvern Hill,
Of Gettysburg and Chancellorsville,
The men whose wasted figures fill
The patriot graves of the nation.

And there came the nameless dead, the men
Who perished in fever swamp and fen,
The slowly-starved of the prison pen;
And, marching beside the others,
Came the dusky martyrs of Pillow's fight,
With limbs enfranchised and bearing bright;
I thought perhaps 'twas the pale moonlight
They looked as white as their brothers!

And so all night marched the nation's dead,
With never a banner above them spread,

Nor a badge, nor a motto brandished;
No mark, save the bare uncovered head
Of the silent bronze Reviewer;
With never an arch save the vaulted sky;
With never a flower save those that lie
On the distant graves, for love could buy
No gift that was purer or truer.

So all night long swept the strange array,
So all night long till the morning gray
I watched for one who had passed away;
With a reverent awe and wonder,
Till a blue cap waved in the length'ning line,
And I knew that one who was kin of mine
Had come; and I spake and lo! that sign
Awakened me from my slumber.

THE COPPERHEAD

(1864)

There is peace in the swamp where the Copperhead sleeps,
Where the waters are stagnant, the white vapor creeps,
Where the musk of Magnolia hangs thick in the air,
And the lilies' phylacteries broaden in prayer.
There is peace in the swamp, though the quiet is death,
Though the mist is miasma, the upas-tree's breath,
Though no echo awakes to the cooing of doves,
There is peace: yes, the peace that the Copperhead loves.

Go seek him: he coils in the ooze and the drip,
Like a thong idly flung from the slave-driver's whip;
But beware the false footstep, the stumble that brings
A deadlier lash than the overseer swings.
Never arrow so true, never bullet so dread,
As the straight steady stroke of that hammer-shaped head;
Whether slave or proud planter, who braves that dull crest,
Woe to him who shall trouble the Copperhead's rest!

Then why waste your labors, brave hearts and strong men,
In tracking a trail to the Copperhead's den?
Lay your axe to the cypress, hew open the shade
To the free sky and sunshine Jehovah has made;
Let the breeze of the North sweep the vapors away,
Till the stagnant lake ripples, the freed waters play;
And then to your heel can you righteously doom
The Copperhead born of its shadow and gloom!

Last night, above the whistling wind,
I heard the welcome rain,
A fusillade upon the roof,
A tattoo on the pane:
The keyhole piped; the chimney-top
A warlike trumpet blew;
Yet, mingling with these sounds of strife,
A softer voice stole through.

"Give thanks, O brothers!" said the voice,
"That He who sent the rains
Hath spared your fields the scarlet dew
That drips from patriot veins:
I've seen the grass on Eastern graves
In brighter verdure rise;
But, oh! the rain that gave it life
Sprang first from human eyes.

"I come to wash away no stain
Upon your wasted lea;
I raise no banners, save the ones
The forest waves to me:
Upon the mountain side, where Spring
Her farthest picket sets,
My reveille awakes a host
Of grassy bayonets.

"I visit every humble roof;
I mingle with the low:
Only upon the highest peaks
My blessings fall in snow;
Until, in tricklings of the stream
And drainings of the lea,
My unspent bounty comes at last
To mingle with the sea."

And thus all night, above the wind,
I heard the welcome rain,
A fusillade upon the roof,
A tattoo on the pane:
The keyhole piped; the chimney-top
A warlike trumpet blew;
But, mingling with these sounds of strife,
This hymn of peace stole through.

THE OLD MAJOR EXPLAINS

(RE-UNION, ARMY OF THE POTOMAC, 12TH MAY, 1871)

Well, you see, the fact is, Colonel, I don't know as I can come:
For the farm is not half planted, and there's work to do at home;
And my leg is getting troublesome, it laid me up last fall,
And the doctors, they have cut and hacked, and never found the ball.

And then, for an old man like me, it's not exactly right,
This kind o' playing soldier with no enemy in sight.
"The Union," that was well enough way up to '66;
But this "Re-Union," maybe now it's mixed with politics?

No? Well, you understand it best; but then, you see, my lad,
I'm deacon now, and some might think that the example's bad.
And week from next is Conference.... You said the twelfth of May?
Why, that's the day we broke their line at Spottsylvan-i-a!

Hot work; eh, Colonel, wasn't it? Ye mind that narrow front:
They called it the "Death-Angle"! Well, well, my lad, we won't
Fight that old battle over now: I only meant to say
I really can't engage to come upon the twelfth of May.

How's Thompson? What! will he be there? Well, now I want to know!
The first man in the rebel works! they called him "Swearing Joe."
A wild young fellow, sir, I fear the rascal was; but then
Well, short of heaven, there wa'n't a place he dursn't lead his men.

And Dick, you say, is coming too. And Billy? ah! it's true
We buried him at Gettysburg: I mind the spot; do you?
A little field below the hill, it must be green this May;
Perhaps that's why the fields about bring him to me to-day.

Well, well, excuse me, Colonel! but there are some things that drop
The tail-board out one's feelings; and the only way's to stop.
So they want to see the old man; ah, the rascals! do they, eh?
Well, I've business down in Boston about the twelfth of May.

CALIFORNIA'S GREETING TO SEWARD

(1869)

We know him well: no need of praise
Or bonfire from the windy hill
To light to softer paths and ways
The world-worn man we honor still.

No need to quote the truths he spoke
That burned through years of war and shame,

While History carves with surer stroke
Across our map his noonday fame.

No need to bid him show the scars
Of blows dealt by the Scaean gate,
Who lived to pass its shattered bars,
And see the foe capitulate:

Who lived to turn his slower feet
Toward the western setting sun,
To see his harvest all complete,
His dream fulfilled, his duty done,

The one flag streaming from the pole,
The one faith borne from sea to sea:
For such a triumph, and such goal,
Poor must our human greeting be.

Ah! rather that the conscious land
In simpler ways salute the Man,
The tall pines bowing where they stand,
The bared head of El Capitan!

The tumult of the waterfalls,
Pohono's kerchief in the breeze,
The waving from the rocky walls,
The stir and rustle of the trees;

Till, lapped in sunset skies of hope,
In sunset lands by sunset seas,
The Young World's Premier treads the slope
Of sunset years in calm and peace.

THE AGED STRANGER

AN INCIDENT OF THE WAR

"I was with Grant" the stranger said;
Said the farmer, "Say no more,
But rest thee here at my cottage porch,
For thy feet are weary and sore."

"I was with Grant" the stranger said;
Said the farmer, "Nay, no more,
I prithee sit at my frugal board,
And eat of my humble store.

"How fares my boy, my soldier boy,
Of the old Ninth Army Corps?

I warrant he bore him gallantly
In the smoke and the battle's roar!"

"I know him not," said the aged man,
"And, as I remarked before,
I was with Grant" - "Nay, nay, I know,"
Said the farmer, "say no more:

"He fell in battle, I see, alas!
Thou'dst smooth these tidings o'er,
Nay, speak the truth, whatever it be,
Though it rend my bosom's core.

"How fell he? With his face to the foe,
Upholding the flag he bore?
Oh, say not that my boy disgraced
The uniform that he wore!"

"I cannot tell," said the aged man,
"And should have remarked before.
That I was with Grant, in Illinois,
Some three years before the war."

Then the farmer spake him never a word,
But beat with his fist full sore
That aged man who had worked for Grant
Some three years before the war.

THE IDYL OF BATTLE HOLLOW

(WAR OF THE REBELLION, 1884)

No, I won't, thar, now, so! And it ain't nothin', no!
And thar's nary to tell that you folks yer don't know;
And it's "Belle, tell us, do!" and it's "Belle, is it true?"
And "Wot's this yer yarn of the Major and you?"
Till I'm sick of it all, so I am, but I s'pose
Thet is nothin' to you.... Well, then, listen! yer goes!

It was after the fight, and around us all night
Thar was poppin' and shootin' a powerful sight;
And the niggers had fled, and Aunt Chlo was abed,
And Pinky and Milly were hid in the shed:
And I ran out at daybreak, and nothin' was nigh
But the growlin' of cannon low down in the sky.

And I saw not a thing, as I ran to the spring,
But a splintered fence rail and a broken-down swing,
And a bird said "Kerchee!" as it sat on a tree,

As if it was lonesome, and glad to see me;
And I filled up my pail and was risin' to go,
When up comes the Major a-canterin' slow.

When he saw me he drew in his reins, and then threw
On the gate-post his bridle, and what does he do
But come down where I sat; and he lifted his hat,
And he says, well, thar ain't any need to tell THAT;
'Twas some foolishness, sure, but it 'mounted to this,
Thet he asked for a drink, and he wanted a kiss.

Then I said (I was mad), "For the water, my lad,
You're too big and must stoop; for a kiss, it's as bad,
You ain't near big enough." And I turned in a huff,
When that Major he laid his white hand on my cuff,
And he says, "You're a trump! Take my pistol, don't fear!
But shoot the next man that insults you, my dear."

Then he stooped to the pool, very quiet and cool,
Leavin' me with that pistol stuck there like a fool,
When thar flashed on my sight a quick glimmer of light
From the top of the little stone fence on the right,
And I knew 'twas a rifle, and back of it all
Rose the face of that bushwhacker, Cherokee Hall!

Then I felt in my dread that the moment the head
Of the Major was lifted, the Major was dead;
And I stood still and white, but Lord! gals, in spite
Of my care, that derned pistol went off in my fright!
Went off, true as gospil! and, strangest of all,
It actooally injured that Cherokee Hall!

Thet's all, now, go 'long! Yes, some folks thinks it's wrong,
And thar's some wants to know to what side I belong;
But I says, "Served him right!" and I go, all my might,
In love or in war, for a fair stand-up fight;
And as for the Major, sho! gals, don't you know
Thet Lord! thar's his step in the garden below.

CALDWELL OF SPRINGFIELD

(NEW JERSEY, 1780)

Here's the spot. Look around you. Above on the height
Lay the Hessians encamped. By that church on the right
Stood the gaunt Jersey farmers. And here ran a wall,
You may dig anywhere and you'll turn up a ball.
Nothing more. Grasses spring, waters run, flowers blow,
Pretty much as they did ninety-three years ago.

Nothing more, did I say? Stay one moment: you've heard
Of Caldwell, the parson, who once preached the word
Down at Springfield? What, no? Come, that's bad; why, he had
All the Jerseys aflame! And they gave him the name
Of the "rebel high priest." He stuck in their gorge,
For he loved the Lord God and he hated King George!

He had cause, you might say! When the Hessians that day
Marched up with Knyphausen, they stopped on their way
At the "farms," where his wife, with a child in her arms,
Sat alone in the house. How it happened none knew
But God and that one of the hireling crew
Who fired the shot! Enough! there she lay,
And Caldwell, the chaplain, her husband, away!

Did he preach, did he pray? Think of him as you stand
By the old church to-day, think of him and his band
Of militant ploughboys! See the smoke and the heat
Of that reckless advance, of that straggling retreat!
Keep the ghost of that wife, foully slain, in your view
And what could you, what should you, what would YOU do?

Why, just what HE did! They were left in the lurch
For the want of more wadding. He ran to the church,
Broke the door, stripped the pews, and dashed out in the road
With his arms full of hymn-books, and threw down his load
At their feet! Then above all the shouting and shots
Rang his voice: "Put Watts into 'em! Boys, give 'em Watts!"

And they did. That is all. Grasses spring, flowers blow,
Pretty much as they did ninety-three years ago.
You may dig anywhere and you'll turn up a ball
But not always a hero like this and that's all.

POEM

DELIVERED ON THE FOURTEENTH ANNIVERSARY OF CALIFORNIA'S ADMISSION INTO THE UNION,
SEPTEMBER 9, 1864

We meet in peace, though from our native East
The sun that sparkles on our birthday feast
Glanced as he rose on fields whose dews were red
With darker tints than those Aurora spread.
Though shorn his rays, his welcome disk concealed
In the dim smoke that veiled each battlefield,
Still striving upward, in meridian pride,
He climbed the walls that East and West divide,
Saw his bright face flashed back from golden sand,

And sapphire seas that lave the Western land.

Strange was the contrast that such scenes disclose
From his high vantage o'er eternal snows;
There War's alarm the brazen trumpet rings
Here his love-song the mailed cicala sings;
There bayonets glitter through the forest glades
Here yellow cornfields stack their peaceful blades;
There the deep trench where Valor finds a grave
Here the long ditch that curbs the peaceful wave;
There the bold sapper with his lighted train
Here the dark tunnel and its stores of gain;
Here the full harvest and the wain's advance
There the Grim Reaper and the ambulance.

With scenes so adverse, what mysterious bond
Links our fair fortunes to the shores beyond?
Why come we here, last of a scattered fold
To pour new metal in the broken mould?
To yield our tribute, stamped with Caesar's face,
To Caesar, stricken in the market-place?

Ah! love of country is the secret tie
That joins these contrasts 'neath one arching sky;
Though brighter paths our peaceful steps explore,
We meet together at the Nation's door.
War winds her horn, and giant cliffs go down
Like the high walls that girt the sacred town,
And bares the pathway to her throbbing heart,
From clustered village and from crowded mart.

Part of God's providence it was to found
A Nation's bulwark on this chosen ground;
Not Jesuit's zeal nor pioneer's unrest
Planted these pickets in the distant West,
But He who first the Nation's fate forecast
Placed here His fountains sealed for ages past,
Rock-ribbed and guarded till the coming time
Should fit the people for their work sublime;
When a new Moses with his rod of steel
Smote the tall cliffs with one wide-ringing peal,
And the old miracle in record told
To the new Nation was revealed in gold.

Judge not too idly that our toils are mean,
Though no new levies marshal on our green;
Nor deem too rashly that our gains are small,
Weighed with the prizes for which heroes fall.
See, where thick vapor wreathes the battle-line;
There Mercy follows with her oil and wine;
Or where brown Labor with its peaceful charm

Stiffens the sinews of the Nation's arm.
What nerves its hands to strike a deadlier blow
And hurl its legions on the rebel foe?
Lo! for each town new rising o'er our State
See the foe's hamlet waste and desolate,
While each new factory lifts its chimney tall,
Like a fresh mortar trained on Richmond's wall.

For this, O brothers, swings the fruitful vine,
Spread our broad pastures with their countless kine:
For this o'erhead the arching vault springs clear,
Sunlit and cloudless for one half the year;
For this no snowflake, e'er so lightly pressed,
Chills the warm impulse of our mother's breast.
Quick to reply, from meadows brown and sere,
She thrills responsive to Spring's earliest tear;
Breaks into blossom, flings her loveliest rose
Ere the white crocus mounts Atlantic snows;
And the example of her liberal creed
Teaches the lesson that to-day we heed.

Thus ours the lot with peaceful, generous hand
To spread our bounty o'er the suffering land;
As the deep cleft in Mariposa's wall
Hurls a vast river splintering in its fall,
Though the rapt soul who stands in awe below
Sees but the arching of the promised bow,
Lo! the far streamlet drinks its dews unseen,
And the whole valley wakes a brighter green.

MISS BLANCHE SAYS

And you are the poet, and so you want
Something, what is it? a theme, a fancy?
Something or other the Muse won't grant
To your old poetical necromancy;
Why, one half you poets, you can't deny
Don't know the Muse when you chance to meet her,
But sit in your attics and mope and sigh
For a faineant goddess to drop from the sky,
When flesh and blood may be standing by
Quite at your service, should you but greet her.

What if I told you my own romance?
Women are poets, if you so take them,
One third poet, the rest what chance
Of man and marriage may choose to make them.
Give me ten minutes before you go,
Here at the window we'll sit together,

Watching the currents that ebb and flow;
Watching the world as it drifts below
Up the hot Avenue's dusty glow:
Isn't it pleasant, this bright June weather?

Well, it was after the war broke out,
And I was a schoolgirl fresh from Paris;
Papa had contracts, and roamed about,
And I did nothing for I was an heiress.
Picked some lint, now I think; perhaps
Knitted some stockings, a dozen nearly:
Havelocks made for the soldiers' caps;
Stood at fair-tables and peddled traps
Quite at a profit. The "shoulder-straps"
Thought I was pretty. Ah, thank you! really?

Still it was stupid. Rata-tat-tat!
Those were the sounds of that battle summer,
Till the earth seemed a parchment round and flat,
And every footfall the tap of a drummer;
And day by day down the Avenue went
Cavalry, infantry, all together,
Till my pitying angel one day sent
My fate in the shape of a regiment,
That halted, just as the day was spent,
Here at our door in the bright June weather.

None of your dandy warriors they,
Men from the West, but where I know not;
Haggard and travel-stained, worn and gray,
With never a ribbon or lace or bow-knot:
And I opened the window, and, leaning there,
I felt in their presence the free winds blowing.
My neck and shoulders and arms were bare,
I did not dream they might think me fair,
But I had some flowers that night in my hair,
And here, on my bosom, a red rose glowing.

And I looked from the window along the line,
Dusty and dirty and grim and solemn,
Till an eye like a bayonet flash met mine,
And a dark face shone from the darkening column,
And a quick flame leaped to my eyes and hair,
Till cheeks and shoulders burned all together,
And the next I found myself standing there
With my eyelids wet and my cheeks less fair,
And the rose from my bosom tossed high in air,
Like a blood-drop falling on plume and feather.

Then I drew back quickly: there came a cheer,
A rush of figures, a noise and tussle,

And then it was over, and high and clear
My red rose bloomed on his gun's black muzzle.
Then far in the darkness a sharp voice cried,
And slowly and steadily, all together,
Shoulder to shoulder and side to side,
Rising and falling and swaying wide,
But bearing above them the rose, my pride,
They marched away in the twilight weather.

And I leaned from my window and watched my rose
Tossed on the waves of the surging column,
Warmed from above in the sunset glows,
Borne from below by an impulse solemn.
Then I shut the window. I heard no more
Of my soldier friend, nor my flower neither,
But lived my life as I did before.
I did not go as a nurse to the war,
Sick folks to me are a dreadful bore,
So I didn't go to the hospital either.

You smile, O poet, and what do you?
You lean from your window, and watch life's column
Trampling and struggling through dust and dew,
Filled with its purposes grave and solemn;
And an act, a gesture, a face, who knows?
Touches your fancy to thrill and haunt you,
And you pluck from your bosom the verse that grows
And down it flies like my red, red rose,
And you sit and dream as away it goes,
And think that your duty is done, now don't you?

I know your answer. I'm not yet through.
Look at this photograph, "In the Trenches"!
That dead man in the coat of blue
Holds a withered rose in his hand. That clenches
Nothing! except that the sun paints true,
And a woman is sometimes prophetic-minded.
And that's my romance. And, poet, you
Take it and mould it to suit your view;
And who knows but you may find it too
Come to your heart once more, as mine did.

AN ARCTIC VISION

Where the short-legged Esquimaux
Waddle in the ice and snow,
And the playful Polar bear
Nips the hunter unaware;
Where by day they track the ermine,

And by night another vermin,
Segment of the frigid zone,
Where the temperature alone
Warms on St. Elias' cone;
Polar dock, where Nature slips
From the ways her icy ships;
Land of fox and deer and sable,
Shore end of our western cable,
Let the news that flying goes
Thrill through all your Arctic floes,
And reverberate the boast
From the cliffs off Beechey's coast,
Till the tidings, circling round
Every bay of Norton Sound,
Throw the vocal tide-wave back
To the isles of Kodiac.
Let the stately Polar bears
Waltz around the pole in pairs,
And the walrus, in his glee,
Bare his tusk of ivory;
While the bold sea-unicorn
Calmly takes an extra horn;
All ye Polar skies, reveal your
Very rarest of parhelia;
Trip it, all ye merry dancers,
In the airiest of "Lancers;"
Slide, ye solemn glaciers, slide,
One inch farther to the tide,
Nor in rash precipitation
Upset Tyndall's calculation.
Know you not what fate awaits you,
Or to whom the future mates you?
All ye icebergs, make salaam,
You belong to Uncle Sam!

On the spot where Eugene Sue
Led his wretched Wandering Jew,
Stands a form whose features strike
Russ and Esquimaux alike.
He it is whom Skalds of old
In their Runic rhymes foretold;
Lean of flank and lank of jaw,
See the real Northern Thor!
See the awful Yankee leering
Just across the Straits of Behring;
On the drifted snow, too plain,
Sinks his fresh tobacco stain,
Just beside the deep inden-
Tation of his Number 10.

Leaning on his icy hammer

Stands the hero of this drama,
And above the wild-duck's clamor,
In his own peculiar grammar,
With its linguistic disguises,
La! the Arctic prologue rises:
"Wall, I reckon 'tain't so bad,
Seein' ez 'twas all they had.

True, the Springs are rather late,
And early Falls predominate;
But the ice-crop's pretty sure,
And the air is kind o' pure;
'Tain't so very mean a trade,
When the land is all surveyed.
There's a right smart chance for fur-chase
All along this recent purchase,
And, unless the stories fail,
Every fish from cod to whale;
Rocks, too; mebbe quartz; let's see,
'Twould be strange if there should be,
Seems I've heerd such stories told;
Eh! why, bless us, yes, it's gold!"

While the blows are falling thick
From his California pick,
You may recognize the Thor
Of the vision that I saw,
Freed from legendary glamour,
See the real magician's hammer.

ST. THOMAS

(A GEOGRAPHICAL SURVEY, 1868)

Very fair and full of promise
Lay the island of St. Thomas:
Ocean o'er its reefs and bars
Hid its elemental scars;
Groves of cocoanut and guava
Grew above its fields of lava.
So the gem of the Antilles
"Isles of Eden," where no ill is
Like a great green turtle slumbered
On the sea that it encumbered.

Then said William Henry Seward,
As he cast his eye to leeward,
"Quite important to our commerce
Is this island of St. Thomas."

Said the Mountain ranges, "Thank'ee,
But we cannot stand the Yankee
O'er our scars and fissures poring,
In our very vitals boring,
In our sacred caverns prying,
All our secret problems trying,
Digging, blasting, with dynamit
Mocking all our thunders! Damn it!
Other lands may be more civil;
Bust our lava crust if we will!"

Said the Sea, its white teeth gnashing
Through its coral-reef lips flashing,
"Shall I let this scheming mortal
Shut with stone my shining portal,
Curb my tide and check my play,
Fence with wharves my shining bay?
Rather let me be drawn out
In one awful waterspout!"

Said the black-browed Hurricane,
Brooding down the Spanish Main,
"Shall I see my forces, zounds!
Measured by square inch and pounds,
With detectives at my back
When I double on my track,
And my secret paths made clear,
Published o'er the hemisphere
To each gaping, prying crew?
Shall I? Blow me if I do!"

So the Mountains shook and thundered,
And the Hurricane came sweeping,
And the people stared and wondered
As the Sea came on them leaping:
Each, according to his promise,
Made things lively at St. Thomas.

Till one morn, when Mr. Seward
Cast his weather eye to leeward,
There was not an inch of dry land
Left to mark his recent island.
Not a flagstaff or a sentry,
Not a wharf or port of entry,
Only to cut matters shorter
Just a patch of muddy water
In the open ocean lying,
And a gull above it flying.

OFF SCARBOROUGH

(SEPTEMBER, 1779)

I

"Have a care!" the bailiffs cried
From their cockleshell that lay
Off the frigate's yellow side,
Tossing on Scarborough Bay,
While the forty sail it convoyed on a bowline stretched away.
"Take your chicks beneath your wings,
And your claws and feathers spread,
Ere the hawk upon them springs,
Ere around Flamborough Head
Swoops Paul Jones, the Yankee falcon, with his beak and talons red."

II

How we laughed! my mate and I,
On the "Bon Homme Richard's" deck,
As we saw that convoy fly
Like a snow-squall, till each fleck
Melted in the twilight shadows of the coast-line, speck by speck;
And scuffling back to shore
The Scarborough bailiffs sped,
As the "Richard" with a roar
Of her cannon round the Head,
Crossed her royal yards and signaled to her consort: "Chase ahead"

III

But the devil seize Landais
In that consort ship of France!
For the shabby, lubber way
That he worked the "Alliance"
In the offing, nor a broadside fired save to our mischance!
When tumbling to the van,
With his battle-lanterns set,
Rose the burly Englishman
'Gainst our hull as black as jet,
Rode the yellow-sided "Serapis," and all alone we met!

IV

All alone, though far at sea
Hung his consort, rounding to;
All alone, though on our lee
Fought our "Pallas," stanch and true!
For the first broadside around us both a smoky circle drew:

And, like champions in a ring,
There was cleared a little space
Scarce a cable's length to swing
Ere we grappled in embrace,
All the world shut out around us, and we only face to face!

V

Then awoke all hell below
From that broadside, doubly curst,
For our long eighteens in row
Leaped the first discharge and burst!
And on deck our men came pouring, fearing their own guns the worst.
And as dumb we lay, till, through
Smoke and flame and bitter cry,
Hailed the "Serapis:" "Have you
Struck your colors?" Our reply,
"We have not yet begun to fight!" went shouting to the sky!

VI

Roux of Brest, old fisher, lay
Like a herring gasping here;
Bunker of Nantucket Bay,
Blown from out the port, dropped sheer
Half a cable's length to leeward; yet we faintly raised a cheer
As with his own right hand
Our Commodore made fast
The foeman's head-gear and
The "Richard's" mizzen-mast,
And in that death-lock clinging held us there from first to last!

VII

Yet the foeman, gun on gun,
Through the "Richard" tore a road,
With his gunners' rammers run
Through our ports at every load,
Till clear the blue beyond us through our yawning timbers showed.
Yet with entrails torn we clung
Like the Spartan to our fox,
And on deck no coward tongue
Wailed the enemy's hard knocks,
Nor that all below us trembled like a wreck upon the rocks.

VIII

Then a thought rose in my brain,
As through Channel mists the sun.
From our tops a fire like rain
Drove below decks every one

Of the enemy's ship's company to hide or work a gun:
And that thought took shape as I
On the "Richard's" yard lay out,
That a man might do and die,
If the doing brought about
Freedom for his home and country, and his messmates' cheering shout!

IX

Then I crept out in the dark
Till I hung above the hatch
Of the "Serapis," a mark
For her marksmen! with a match
And a hand-grenade, but lingered just a moment more to snatch
One last look at sea and sky!
At the lighthouse on the hill!
At the harvest-moon on high!
And our pine flag fluttering still!
Then turned and down her yawning throat I launched that devil's pill!

X

Then a blank was all between
As the flames around me spun!
Had I fired the magazine?
Was the victory lost or won?
Nor knew I till the fight was o'er but half my work was done:
For I lay among the dead
In the cockpit of our foe,
With a roar above my head,
Till a trampling to and fro,
And a lantern showed my mate's face, and I knew what now you know!

CADET GREY

CANTO I

I

Act first, scene first. A study. Of a kind
Half cell, half salon, opulent yet grave;
Rare books, low-shelved, yet far above the mind
Of common man to compass or to crave;
Some slight relief of pamphlets that inclined
The soul at first to trifling, till, dismayed
By text and title, it drew back resigned,
Nor cared with levity to vex a shade
That to itself such perfect concord made.

II

Some thoughts like these perplexed the patriot brain
Of Jones, Lawgiver to the Commonwealth,
As on the threshold of this chaste domain
He paused expectant, and looked up in stealth
To darkened canvases that frowned amain,
With stern-eyed Puritans, who first began
To spread their roots in Georgius Primus' reign,
Nor dropped till now, obedient to some plan,
Their century fruit, the perfect Boston man.

III

Somewhere within that Russia-scented gloom
A voice catarrhal thrilled the Member's ear:
"Brief is our business, Jones. Look round this room!
Regard yon portraits! Read their meaning clear!
These much proclaim MY station. I presume
YOU are our Congressman, before whose wit
And sober judgment shall the youth appear
Who for West Point is deemed most just and fit
To serve his country and to honor it."

IV

"Such is my son! Elsewhere perhaps 'twere wise
Trial competitive should guide your choice.
There are some people I can well surmise
Themselves must show their merits. History's voice
Spares me that trouble: all desert that lies
In yonder ancestor of Queen Anne's day,
Or yon grave Governor, is all my boy's,
Reverts to him; entailed, as one might say;
In brief, result in Winthrop Adams Grey!"

V

He turned and laid his well-bred hand, and smiled,
On the cropped head of one who stood beside.
Ah me! in sooth it was no ruddy child
Nor brawny youth that thrilled the father's pride;
'Twas but a Mind that somehow had beguiled
From soulless Matter processes that served
For speech and motion and digestion mild,
Content if all one moral purpose nerved,
Nor recked thereby its spine were somewhat curved.

VI

He was scarce eighteen. Yet ere he was eight

He had despoiled the classics; much he knew
Of Sanskrit; not that he placed undue weight
On this, but that it helped him with Hebrew,
His favorite tongue. He learned, alas! too late,
One can't begin too early, would regret
That boyish whim to ascertain the state
Of Venus' atmosphere made him forget
That philologic goal on which his soul was set.

VII

He too had traveled; at the age of ten
Found Paris empty, dull except for art
And accent. "Mabille" with its glories then
Less than Egyptian "Almees" touched a heart
Nothing if not pure classic. If some men
Thought him a prig, it vexed not his conceit,
But moved his pity, and ofttimes his pen,
The better to instruct them, through some sheet
Published in Boston, and signed "Beacon Street."

VIII

From premises so plain the blind could see
But one deduction, and it came next day.
"In times like these, the very name of G.
Speaks volumes," wrote the Honorable J.
"Inclosed please find appointment." Presently
Came a reception to which Harvard lent
Fourteen professors, and, to give esprit,
The Liberal Club some eighteen ladies sent,
Five that spoke Greek, and thirteen sentiment.

IX

Four poets came who loved each other's song,
And two philosophers, who thought that they
Were in most things impractical and wrong;
And two reformers, each in his own way
Peculiar, one who had waxed strong
On herbs and water, and such simple fare;
Two foreign lions, "Ram See" and "Chy Long,"
And several artists claimed attention there,
Based on the fact they had been snubbed elsewhere.

X

With this indorsement nothing now remained
But counsel, Godspeed, and some calm adieux;
No foolish tear the father's eyelash stained,
And Winthrop's cheek as guiltless shone of dew.

A slight publicity, such as obtained
In classic Rome, these few last hours attended.
The day arrived, the train and depot gained,
The mayor's own presence this last act commended
The train moved off and here the first act ended.

CANTO II

I

Where West Point crouches, and with lifted shield
Turns the whole river eastward through the pass;
Whose jutting crags, half silver, stand revealed
Like bossy bucklers of Leonidas;
Where buttressed low against the storms that wield
Their summer lightnings where her eaglets swarm,
By Freedom's cradle Nature's self has steeled
Her heart, like Winkelried, and to that storm
Of leveled lances bares her bosom warm.

II

But not to-night. The air and woods are still,
The faintest rustle in the trees below,
The lowest tremor from the mountain rill,
Come to the ear as but the trailing flow
Of spirit robes that walk unseen the hill;
The moon low sailing o'er the upland farm,
The moon low sailing where the waters fill
The lozenge lake, beside the banks of balm,
Gleams like a chevron on the river's arm.

III

All space breathes languor: from the hilltop high,
Where Putnam's bastion crumbles in the past,
To swooning depths where drowsy cannon lie
And wide-mouthed mortars gape in slumbers vast;
Stroke upon stroke, the far oars glance and die
On the hushed bosom of the sleeping stream;
Bright for one moment drifts a white sail by,
Bright for one moment shows a bayonet gleam
Far on the level plain, then passes as a dream.

IV

Soft down the line of darkened battlements,
Bright on each lattice of the barrack walls,
Where the low arching sallyport indents,
Seen through its gloom beyond, the moonbeam falls.

All is repose save where the camping tents
Mock the white gravestones farther on, where sound
No morning guns for reveille, nor whence
No drum-beat calls retreat, but still is ever found
Waiting and present on each sentry's round.

V

Within the camp they lie, the young, the brave,
Half knight, half schoolboy, acolytes of fame,
Pledged to one altar, and perchance one grave;
Bred to fear nothing but reproach and blame,
Ascetic dandies o'er whom vestals rave,
Clean-limbed young Spartans, disciplined young elves,
Taught to destroy, that they may live to save,
Students embattled, soldiers at their shelves,
Heroes whose conquests are at first themselves.

VI

Within the camp they lie, in dreams are freed
From the grim discipline they learn to love;
In dreams no more the sentry's challenge heed,
In dreams afar beyond their pickets rove;
One treads once more the piny paths that lead
To his green mountain home, and pausing hears
The cattle call; one treads the tangled weed
Of slippery rocks beside Atlantic piers;
One smiles in sleep, one wakens wet with tears.

VII

One scents the breath of jasmine flowers that twine
The pillared porches of his Southern home;
One hears the coo of pigeons in the pine
Of Western woods where he was wont to roam;
One sees the sunset fire the distant line
Where the long prairie sweeps its levels down;
One treads the snow-peaks; one by lamps that shine
Down the broad highways of the sea-girt town;
And two are missing, Cadets Grey and Brown!

VIII

Much as I grieve to chronicle the fact,
That selfsame truant known as "Cadet Grey"
Was the young hero of our moral tract,
Shorn of his twofold names on entrance-day.
"Winthrop" and "Adams" dropped in that one act
Of martial curtness, and the roll-call thinned
Of his ancestors, he with youthful tact

Indulgence claimed, since Winthrop no more sinned,
Nor sainted Adams winced when he, plain Grey, was "skinned."

IX

He had known trials since we saw him last,
By sheer good luck had just escaped rejection,
Not for his learning, but that it was cast
In a spare frame scarce fit for drill inspection;
But when he ope'd his lips a stream so vast
Of information flooded each professor,
They quite forgot his eyeglass, something past
All precedent, accepting the transgressor,
Weak eyes and all of which he was possessor.

X

E'en the first day he touched a blackboard's space
So the tradition of his glory lingers
Two wise professors fainted, each with face
White as the chalk within his rapid fingers:
All day he ciphered, at such frantic pace,
His form was hid in chalk precipitation
Of every problem, till they said his case
Could meet from them no fair examination
Till Congress made a new appropriation.

XI

Famous in molecules, he demonstrated
From the mess hash to many a listening classful;
Great as a botanist, he separated
Three kinds of "Mentha" in one julep's glassful;
High in astronomy, it has been stated
He was the first at West Point to discover
Mars' missing satellites, and calculated
Their true positions, not the heavens over,
But 'neath the window of Miss Kitty Rover.

XII

Indeed, I fear this novelty celestial
That very night was visible and clear;
At least two youths of aspect most terrestrial,
And clad in uniform, were loitering near
A villa's casement, where a gentle vestal
Took their impatience somewhat patiently,
Knowing the youths were somewhat green and "bestial"
(A certain slang of the Academy,
I beg the reader won't refer to me).

XIII

For when they ceased their ardent strain, Miss Kitty
Glowed not with anger nor a kindred flame,
But rather flushed with an odd sort of pity,
Half matron's kindness, and half coquette's shame;
Proud yet quite blameful, when she heard their ditty
She gave her soul poetical expression,
And being clever too, as she was pretty,
From her high casement warbled this confession,
Half provocation and one half repression:

NOT YET

Not yet, O friend, not yet! the patient stars
Lean from their lattices, content to wait.
All is illusion till the morning bars
Slip from the levels of the Eastern gate.
Night is too young, O friend! day is too near;
Wait for the day that maketh all things clear.
Not yet, O friend, not yet!

Not yet, O love, not yet! all is not true,
All is not ever as it seemeth now.
Soon shall the river take another blue,
Soon dies yon light upon the mountain brow.
What lieth dark, O love, bright day will fill;
Wait for thy morning, be it good or ill.
Not yet, O love, not yet!

XIV

The strain was finished; softly as the night
Her voice died from the window, yet e'en then
Fluttered and fell likewise a kerchief white;
But that no doubt was accident, for when
She sought her couch she deemed her conduct quite
Beyond the reach of scandalous commenter,
Washing her hands of either gallant wight,
Knowing the moralist might compliment her,
Thus voicing Siren with the words of Mentor.

XV

She little knew the youths below, who straight
Dived for her kerchief, and quite overlooked
The pregnant moral she would inculcate;
Nor dreamed the less how little Winthrop brooked

Her right to doubt his soul's maturer state.
Brown, who was Western, amiable, and new
Might take the moral and accept his fate;
The which he did, but, being stronger too,
Took the white kerchief, also, as his due.

XVI

They did not quarrel, which no doubt seemed queer
To those who knew not how their friendship blended;
Each was opposed, and each the other's peer,
Yet each the other in some things transcended.
Where Brown lacked culture, brains, and oft, I fear,
Cash in his pocket, Grey of course supplied him;
Where Grey lacked frankness, force, and faith sincere,
Brown of his manhood suffered none to chide him,
But in his faults stood manfully beside him.

XVII

In academic walks and studies grave,
In the camp drill and martial occupation,
They helped each other: but just here I crave
Space for the reader's full imagination,
The fact is patent, Grey became a slave!
A tool, a fag, a "pleb"! To state it plainer,
All that blue blood and ancestry e'er gave
Cleaned guns, brought water! was, in fact, retainer
To Jones, whose uncle was a paper-stainer!

XVIII

How they bore this at home I cannot say:
I only know so runs the gossip's tale.
It chanced one day that the paternal Grey
Came to West Point that he himself might hail
The future hero in some proper way
Consistent with his lineage. With him came
A judge, a poet, and a brave array
Of aunts and uncles, bearing each a name,
Eyeglass and respirator with the same.

XIX

"Observe!" quoth Grey the elder to his friends,
"Not in these giddy youths at baseball playing
You'll notice Winthrop Adams! Greater ends
Than these absorb HIS leisure. No doubt straying
With Caesar's Commentaries, he attends
Some Roman council. Let us ask, however,
Yon grimy urchin, who my soul offends

By wheeling offal, if he will endeavor
To find - What! heaven! Winthrop! Oh! no! never!"

XX

Alas! too true! The last of all the Greys
Was "doing police detail," it had come
To this; in vain the rare historic bays
That crowned the pictured Puritans at home!
And yet 'twas certain that in grosser ways
Of health and physique he was quite improving.
Straighter he stood, and had achieved some praise
In other exercise, much more behooving
A soldier's taste than merely dirt removing.

XXI

But to resume: we left the youthful pair,
Some stanzas back, before a lady's bower;
'Tis to be hoped they were no longer there,
For stars were pointing to the morning hour.
Their escapade discovered, ill 'twould fare
With our two heroes, derelict of orders;
But, like the ghost, they "scent the morning air,"
And back again they steal across the borders,
Unseen, unheeded, by their martial warders.

XXII

They got to bed with speed: young Grey to dream
Of some vague future with a general's star,
And Mistress Kitty basking in its gleam;
While Brown, content to worship her afar,
Dreamed himself dying by some lonely stream,
Having snatched Kitty from eighteen Nez Perces,
Till a far bugle, with the morning beam,
In his dull ear its fateful song rehearses,
Which Winthrop Adams after put to verses.

XXIII

So passed three years of their novitiate,
The first real boyhood Grey had ever known.
His youth ran clear, not choked like his Cochituate,
In civic pipes, but free and pure alone;
Yet knew repression, could himself habituate
To having mind and body well rubbed down,
Could read himself in others, and could situate
Themselves in him, except, I grieve to own,
He couldn't see what Kitty saw in Brown!

XXIV

At last came graduation; Brown received
In the One Hundredth Cavalry commission;
Then frolic, flirting, parting, when none grieved
Save Brown, who loved our young Academician.
And Grey, who felt his friend was still deceived
By Mistress Kitty, who with other beauties
Graced the occasion, and it was believed
Had promised Brown that when he could recruit his
Promised command, she'd share with him those duties.

XXV

Howe'er this was I know not; all I know,
The night was June's, the moon rode high and clear;
"'Twas such a night as this," three years ago,
Miss Kitty sang the song that two might hear.
There is a walk where trees o'erarching grow,
Too wide for one, not wide enough for three
(A fact precluding any plural beau),
Which quite explained Miss Kitty's company,
But not why Grey that favored one should be.

XXVI

There is a spring, whose limpid waters hide
Somewhere within the shadows of that path
Called Kosciusko's. There two figures bide,
Grey and Miss Kitty. Surely Nature hath
No fairer mirror for a might-be bride
Than this same pool that caught our gentle belle
To its dark heart one moment. At her side
Grey bent. A something trembled o'er the well,
Bright, spherical, a tear? Ah no! a button fell!

XXVII

"Material minds might think that gravitation,"
Quoth Grey, "drew yon metallic spheroid down.
The soul poetic views the situation
Fraught with more meaning. When thy girlish crown
Was mirrored there, there was disintegration
Of me, and all my spirit moved to you,
Taking the form of slow precipitation!"
But here came "Taps," a start, a smile, adieu!
A blush, a sigh, and end of Canto II.

BUGLE SONG

Fades the light,

And afar
Goeth day, cometh night;
And a star
Leadeth all,
Speedeth all
To their rest!

Love, good-night!
Must thou go
When the day
And the light
Need thee so,
Needeth all,
Heedeth all,
That is best?

CANTO III

I

Where the sun sinks through leagues of arid sky,
Where the sun dies o'er leagues of arid plain,
Where the dead bones of wasted rivers lie,
Trailed from their channels in yon mountain chain;
Where day by day naught takes the wearied eye
But the low-rimming mountains, sharply based
On the dead levels, moving far or nigh,
As the sick vision wanders o'er the waste,
But ever day by day against the sunset traced:

II

There moving through a poisonous cloud that stings
With dust of alkali the trampling band
Of Indian ponies, ride on dusky wings
The red marauders of the Western land;
Heavy with spoil, they seek the trail that brings
Their flaunting lances to that sheltered bank
Where lie their lodges; and the river sings
Forgetful of the plain beyond, that drank
Its life blood, where the wasted caravan sank.

III

They brought with them the thief's ignoble spoil,
The beggar's dole, the greed of chiffonnier,
The scum of camps, the implements of toil
Snatched from dead hands, to rust as useless here;
All they could rake or glean from hut or soil
Piled their lean ponies, with the jackdaw's greed

For vacant glitter. It were scarce a foil
To all this tinsel that one feathered reed
Bore on its barb two scalps that freshly bleed!

IV

They brought with them, alas! a wounded foe,
Bound hand and foot, yet nursed with cruel care,
Lest that in death he might escape one throe
They had decreed his living flesh should bear:
A youthful officer, by one foul blow
Of treachery surprised, yet fighting still
Amid his ambushed train, calm as the snow
Above him; hopeless, yet content to spill
His blood with theirs, and fighting but to kill.

V

He had fought nobly, and in that brief spell
Had won the awe of those rude border men
Who gathered round him, and beside him fell
In loyal faith and silence, save that when
By smoke embarrassed, and near sight as well,
He paused to wipe his eyeglass, and decide
Its nearer focus, there arose a yell
Of approbation, and Bob Barker cried,
"Wade in, Dundreary!" tossed his cap and died.

VI

Their sole survivor now! his captors bear
Him all unconscious, and beside the stream
Leave him to rest; meantime the squaws prepare
The stake for sacrifice: nor wakes a gleam
Of pity in those Furies' eyes that glare
Expectant of the torture; yet alway
His steadfast spirit shines and mocks them there
With peace they know not, till at close of day
On his dull ear there thrills a whispered "Grey!"

VII

He starts! Was it a trick? Had angels kind
Touched with compassion some weak woman's breast?
Such things he'd read of! Faintly to his mind
Came Pocahontas pleading for her guest.
But then, this voice, though soft, was still inclined
To baritone! A squaw in ragged gown
Stood near him, frowning hatred. Was he blind?
Whose eye was this beneath that beetling frown?
The frown was painted, but that wink meant Brown!

VIII

"Hush! for your life and mine! the thongs are cut,"
He whispers; "in yon thicket stands my horse.
One dash! I follow close, as if to glut
My own revenge, yet bar the others' course.
Now!" And 'tis done. Grey speeds, Brown follows; but
Ere yet they reach the shade, Grey, fainting, reels,
Yet not before Brown's circling arms close shut
His in, uplifting him! Anon he feels
A horse beneath him bound, and hears the rattling heels.

IX

Then rose a yell of baffled hate, and sprang
Headlong the savages in swift pursuit;
Though speed the fugitives, they hope to hang
Hot on their heels, like wolves, with tireless foot.
Long is the chase; Brown hears with inward pang
The short, hard panting of his gallant steed
Beneath its double burden; vainly rang
Both voice and spur. The heaving flanks may bleed,
Yet comes the sequel that they still must heed!

X

Brown saw it, reined his steed; dismounting, stood
Calm and inflexible. "Old chap! you see
There is but ONE escape. You know it? Good!
There is ONE man to take it. You are he.
The horse won't carry double. If he could,
'Twould but protract this bother. I shall stay:
I've business with these devils, they with me;
I will occupy them till you get away.
Hush! quick time, forward. There! God bless you, Grey!"

XI

But as he finished, Grey slipped to his feet,
Calm as his ancestors in voice and eye:
"You do forget yourself when you compete
With him whose RIGHT it is to stay and die:
That's not YOUR duty. Please regain your seat;
And take my ORDERS, since I rank you here!
Mount and rejoin your men, and my defeat
Report at quarters. Take this letter; ne'er
Give it to aught but HER, nor let aught interfere."

XII

And, shamed and blushing, Brown the letter took
Obediently and placed it in his pocket;
Then, drawing forth another, said, "I look
For death as you do, wherefore take this locket
And letter." Here his comrade's hand he shook
In silence. "Should we both together fall,
Some other man" but here all speech forsook
His lips, as ringing cheerily o'er all
He heard afar his own dear bugle-call!

XIII

'Twas his command and succor, but e'en then
Grey fainted, with poor Brown, who had forgot
He likewise had been wounded, and both men
Were picked up quite unconscious of their lot.
Long lay they in extremity, and when
They both grew stronger, and once more exchanged
Old vows and memories, one common "den"
In hospital was theirs, and free they ranged,
Awaiting orders, but no more estranged.

XIV

And yet 'twas strange, nor can I end my tale
Without this moral, to be fair and just:
They never sought to know why each did fail
The prompt fulfillment of the other's trust.
It was suggested they could not avail
Themselves of either letter, since they were
Duly dispatched to their address by mail
By Captain X., who knew Miss Rover fair
Now meant stout Mistress Bloggs of Blank Blank Square.

II. SPANISH IDYLS AND LEGENDS

THE MIRACLE OF PADRE JUNIPERO

This is the tale that the Chronicle
Tells of the wonderful miracle
Wrought by the pious Padre Serro,
The very reverend Junipero.

The heathen stood on his ancient mound,
Looking over the desert bound
Into the distant, hazy South,
Over the dusty and broad champaign,
Where, with many a gaping mouth

And fissure, cracked by the fervid drouth,
For seven months had the wasted plain
Known no moisture of dew or rain.
The wells were empty and choked with sand;
The rivers had perished from the land;
Only the sea-fogs to and fro
Slipped like ghosts of the streams below.
Deep in its bed lay the river's bones,
Bleaching in pebbles and milk-white stones,
And tracked o'er the desert faint and far,
Its ribs shone bright on each sandy bar.

Thus they stood as the sun went down
Over the foot-hills bare and brown;
Thus they looked to the South, wherefrom
The pale-face medicine-man should come,
Not in anger or in strife,
But to bring, so ran the tale
The welcome springs of eternal life,
The living waters that should not fail.

Said one, "He will come like Manitou,
Unseen, unheard, in the falling dew."
Said another, "He will come full soon
Out of the round-faced watery moon."
And another said, "He is here!" and lo,
Faltering, staggering, feeble and slow,
Out from the desert's blinding heat
The Padre dropped at the heathen's feet.

They stood and gazed for a little space
Down on his pallid and careworn face,
And a smile of scorn went round the band
As they touched alternate with foot and hand
This mortal waif, that the outer space
Of dim mysterious sky and sand
Flung with so little of Christian grace
Down on their barren, sterile strand.

Said one to him: "It seems thy God
Is a very pitiful kind of God:
He could not shield thine aching eyes
From the blowing desert sands that rise,
Nor turn aside from thy old gray head
The glittering blade that is brandished
By the sun He set in the heavens high;
He could not moisten thy lips when dry;
The desert fire is in thy brain;
Thy limbs are racked with the fever-pain.
If this be the grace He showeth thee
Who art His servant, what may we,

Strange to His ways and His commands,
Seek at His unforgiving hands?"

"Drink but this cup," said the Padre, straight,
"And thou shalt know whose mercy bore
These aching limbs to your heathen door,
And purged my soul of its gross estate.
Drink in His name, and thou shalt see
The hidden depths of this mystery.
Drink!" and he held the cup. One blow
From the heathen dashed to the ground below
The sacred cup that the Padre bore,
And the thirsty soil drank the precious store
Of sacramental and holy wine,
That emblem and consecrated sign
And blessed symbol of blood divine.

Then, says the legend (and they who doubt
The same as heretics be accurst),
From the dry and feverish soil leaped out
A living fountain; a well-spring burst
Over the dusty and broad champaign,
Over the sandy and sterile plain,
Till the granite ribs and the milk-white stones
That lay in the valley, the scattered bones
Moved in the river and lived again!

Such was the wonderful miracle
Wrought by the cup of wine that fell
From the hands of the pious Padre Serro,
The very reverend Junipero.

THE WONDERFUL SPRING OF SAN JOAQUIN

Of all the fountains that poets sing,
Crystal, thermal, or mineral spring,
Ponce de Leon's Fount of Youth,
Wells with bottoms of doubtful truth,
In short, of all the springs of Time
That ever were flowing in fact or rhyme,
That ever were tasted, felt, or seen,
There were none like the Spring of San Joaquin.

Anno Domini eighteen-seven,
Father Dominguez (now in heaven,
Obiit eighteen twenty-seven)
Found the spring, and found it, too,
By his mule's miraculous cast of a shoe;
For his beast, a descendant of Balaam's ass

Stopped on the instant, and would not pass.

The Padre thought the omen good,
And bent his lips to the trickling flood;
Then as the Chronicles declare,
On the honest faith of a true believer
His cheeks, though wasted, lank, and bare,
Filled like a withered russet pear
In the vacuum of a glass receiver,
And the snows that seventy winters bring
Melted away in that magic spring.

Such, at least, was the wondrous news
The Padre brought into Santa Cruz.
The Church, of course, had its own views
Of who were worthiest to use
The magic spring; but the prior claim
Fell to the aged, sick, and lame.
Far and wide the people came:
Some from the healthful Aptos Creek
Hastened to bring their helpless sick;
Even the fishers of rude Soquel
Suddenly found they were far from well;
The brawny dwellers of San Lorenzo
Said, in fact, they had never been so;
And all were ailing, strange to say,
From Pescadero to Monterey.

Over the mountain they poured in,
With leathern bottles and bags of skin;
Through the canyons a motley throng
Trotted, hobbled, and limped along.
The Fathers gazed at the moving scene
With pious joy and with souls serene;
And then a result perhaps foreseen
They laid out the Mission of San Joaquin.

Not in the eyes of faith alone
The good effects of the water shone;
But skins grew rosy, eyes waxed clear,
Of rough vaquero and muleteer;
Angular forms were rounded out,
Limbs grew supple and waists grew stout;
And as for the girls, for miles about
They had no equal! To this day,
From Pescadero to Monterey,
You'll still find eyes in which are seen
The liquid graces of San Joaquin.

There is a limit to human bliss,
And the Mission of San Joaquin had this;

None went abroad to roam or stay
But they fell sick in the queerest way,
A singular maladie du pays,
With gastric symptoms: so they spent
Their days in a sensuous content,
Caring little for things unseen
Beyond their bowers of living green,
Beyond the mountains that lay between
The world and the Mission of San Joaquin.

Winter passed, and the summer came
The trunks of madrono, all aflame,
Here and there through the underwood
Like pillars of fire starkly stood.
All of the breezy solitude
Was filled with the spicing of pine and bay
And resinous odors mixed and blended;
And dim and ghostlike, far away,
The smoke of the burning woods ascended.
Then of a sudden the mountains swam,
The rivers piled their floods in a dam,
The ridge above Los Gatos Creek
Arched its spine in a feline fashion;
The forests waltzed till they grew sick,
And Nature shook in a speechless passion;
And, swallowed up in the earthquake's spleen,
The wonderful Spring of San Joaquin
Vanished, and never more was seen!

Two days passed: the Mission folk
Out of their rosy dream awoke;
Some of them looked a trifle white,
But that, no doubt, was from earthquake fright.
Three days: there was sore distress,
Headache, nausea, giddiness.
Four days: faintings, tenderness
Of the mouth and fauces; and in less
Than one week, here the story closes;
We won't continue the prognosis
Enough that now no trace is seen
Of Spring or Mission of San Joaquin.

MORAL

You see the point? Don't be too quick
To break bad habits: better stick,
Like the Mission folk, to your ARSENIC.

THE ANGELUS

(HEARD AT THE MISSION DOLORES, 1868)

Bells of the Past, whose long-forgotten music
Still fills the wide expanse,
Tingeing the sober twilight of the Present
With color of romance!

I hear your call, and see the sun descending
On rock and wave and sand,
As down the coast the Mission voices, blending,
Girdle the heathen land.

Within the circle of your incantation
No blight nor mildew falls;
Nor fierce unrest, nor lust, nor low ambition
Passes those airy walls.

Borne on the swell of your long waves receding,
I touch the farther Past;
I see the dying glow of Spanish glory,
The sunset dream and last!

Before me rise the dome-shaped Mission towers,
The white Presidio;
The swart commander in his leathern jerkin,
The priest in stole of snow.

Once more I see Portala's cross uplifting
Above the setting sun;
And past the headland, northward, slowly drifting,
The freighted galleon.

O solemn bells! whose consecrated masses
Recall the faith of old;
O tinkling bells! that lulled with twilight music
The spiritual fold!

Your voices break and falter in the darkness,
Break, falter, and are still;
And veiled and mystic, like the Host descending,
The sun sinks from the hill!

CONCEPCION DE ARGUELLO

(PRESIDIO DE SAN FRANCISCO, 1800)

I

Looking seaward, o'er the sand-hills stands the fortress, old and quaint,
By the San Francisco friars lifted to their patron saint,

Sponsor to that wondrous city, now apostate to the creed,
On whose youthful walls the Padre saw the angel's golden reed;

All its trophies long since scattered, all its blazon brushed away;
And the flag that flies above it but a triumph of to-day.

Never scar of siege or battle challenges the wandering eye,
Never breach of warlike onset holds the curious passer-by;

Only one sweet human fancy interweaves its threads of gold
With the plain and homespun present, and a love that ne'er grows old;

Only one thing holds its crumbling walls above the meaner dust,
Listen to the simple story of a woman's love and trust.

II

Count von Resanoff, the Russian, envoy of the mighty Czar,
Stood beside the deep embrasures, where the brazen cannon are.

He with grave provincial magnates long had held serene debate
On the Treaty of Alliance and the high affairs of state;

He from grave provincial magnates oft had turned to talk apart
With the Commandante's daughter on the questions of the heart,

Until points of gravest import yielded slowly one by one,
And by Love was consummated what Diplomacy begun;

Till beside the deep embrasures, where the brazen cannon are,
He received the twofold contract for approval of the Czar;

Till beside the brazen cannon the betrothed bade adieu,
And from sallyport and gateway north the Russian eagles flew.

III

Long beside the deep embrasures, where the brazen cannon are,
Did they wait the promised bridegroom and the answer of the Czar;

Day by day on wall and bastion beat the hollow, empty breeze,
Day by day the sunlight glittered on the vacant, smiling seas:

Week by week the near hills whitened in their dusty leather cloaks,
Week by week the far hills darkened from the fringing plain of oaks;

Till the rains came, and far breaking, on the fierce southwester tost,
Dashed the whole long coast with color, and then vanished and were

lost.

So each year the seasons shifted, wet and warm and drear and dry
Half a year of clouds and flowers, half a year of dust and sky.

Still it brought no ship nor message, brought no tidings, ill or meet,
For the statesmanlike Commander, for the daughter fair and sweet.

Yet she heard the varying message, voiceless to all ears beside:
"He will come," the flowers whispered; "Come no more," the dry hills sighed.

Still she found him with the waters lifted by the morning breeze,
Still she lost him with the folding of the great white-tented seas;

Until hollows chased the dimples from her cheeks of olive brown,
And at times a swift, shy moisture dragged the long sweet lashes down;

Or the small mouth curved and quivered as for some denied caress,
And the fair young brow was knitted in an infantine distress.

Then the grim Commander, pacing where the brazen cannon are,
Comforted the maid with proverbs, wisdom gathered from afar;

Bits of ancient observation by his fathers garnered, each
As a pebble worn and polished in the current of his speech:

"'Those who wait the coming rider travel twice as far as he;'
'Tired wench and coming butter never did in time agree;'

"'He that getteth himself honey, though a clown, he shall have flies;'
'In the end God grinds the miller;' 'In the dark the mole has eyes;'

"'He whose father is Alcalde of his trial hath no fear,'
And be sure the Count has reasons that will make his conduct clear."

Then the voice sententious faltered, and the wisdom it would teach
Lost itself in fondest trifles of his soft Castilian speech;

And on "Concha" "Conchitita," and "Conchita" he would dwell
With the fond reiteration which the Spaniard knows so well.

So with proverbs and caresses, half in faith and half in doubt,
Every day some hope was kindled, flickered, faded, and went out.

IV

Yearly, down the hillside sweeping, came the stately cavalcade,
Bringing revel to vaquero, joy and comfort to each maid;

Bringing days of formal visit, social feast and rustic sport,
Of bull-baiting on the plaza, of love-making in the court.

Vainly then at Concha's lattice, vainly as the idle wind,
Rose the thin high Spanish tenor that bespoke the youth too kind;

Vainly, leaning from their saddles, caballeros, bold and fleet,
Plucked for her the buried chicken from beneath their mustang's feet;

So in vain the barren hillsides with their gay serapes blazed,
Blazed and vanished in the dust-cloud that their flying hoofs had
raised.

Then the drum called from the rampart, and once more, with patient mien,
The Commander and his daughter each took up the dull routine,

Each took up the petty duties of a life apart and lone,
Till the slow years wrought a music in its dreary monotone.

V

Forty years on wall and bastion swept the hollow idle breeze,
Since the Russian eagle fluttered from the California seas;

Forty years on wall and bastion wrought its slow but sure decay,
And St. George's cross was lifted in the port of Monterey;

And the citadel was lighted, and the hall was gayly drest,
All to honor Sir George Simpson, famous traveler and guest.

Far and near the people gathered to the costly banquet set,
And exchanged congratulations with the English baronet;

Till, the formal speeches ended, and amidst the laugh and wine,
Some one spoke of Concha's lover, heedless of the warning sign.

Quickly then cried Sir George Simpson: "Speak no ill of him, I pray!
He is dead. He died, poor fellow, forty years ago this day,

"Died while speeding home to Russia, falling from a fractious horse.
Left a sweetheart, too, they tell me. Married, I suppose, of course!

"Lives she yet?" A deathlike silence fell on banquet, guests, and
hall,
And a trembling figure rising fixed the awestruck gaze of all.

Two black eyes in darkened orbits gleamed beneath the nun's white hood;
Black serge hid the wasted figure, bowed and stricken where it stood.

"Lives she yet?" Sir George repeated. All were hushed as Concha drew
Closer yet her nun's attire. "Senor, pardon, she died, too!"

"FOR THE KING"

(NORTHERN MEXICO, 1640)

As you look from the plaza at Leon west
You can see her house, but the view is best
From the porch of the church where she lies at rest;

Where much of her past still lives, I think,
In the scowling brows and sidelong blink
Of the worshiping throng that rise or sink

To the waxen saints that, yellow and lank,
Lean out from their niches, rank on rank,
With a bloodless Saviour on either flank;

In the gouty pillars, whose cracks begin
To show the adobe core within,
A soul of earth in a whitewashed skin.

And I think that the moral of all, you'll say,
Is the sculptured legend that moulds away
On a tomb in the choir: "Por el Rey."

"Por el Rey!" Well, the king is gone
Ages ago, and the Hapsburg one
Shot but the Rock of the Church lives on.

"Por el Rey!" What matters, indeed,
If king or president succeed
To a country haggard with sloth and greed,

As long as one granary is fat,
And yonder priest, in a shovel hat,
Peeps out from the bin like a sleek brown rat?

What matters? Naught, if it serves to bring
The legend nearer, no other thing,
We'll spare the moral, "Live the king!"

Two hundred years ago, they say,
The Viceroy, Marquis of Monte-Rey,
Rode with his retinue that way:

Grave, as befitted Spain's grandee;
Grave, as the substitute should be
Of His Most Catholic Majesty;

Yet, from his black plume's curving grace
To his slim black gauntlet's smaller space,

Exquisite as a piece of lace!

Two hundred years ago, e'en so
The Marquis stopped where the lime-trees blow,
While Leon's seneschal bent him low,

And begged that the Marquis would that night take
His humble roof for the royal sake,
And then, as the custom demanded, spake

The usual wish, that his guest would hold
The house, and all that it might enfold,
As his, with the bride scarce three days old.

Be sure that the Marquis, in his place,
Replied to all with the measured grace
Of chosen speech and unmoved face;

Nor raised his head till his black plume swept
The hem of the lady's robe, who kept
Her place, as her husband backward stept.

And then (I know not how nor why)
A subtle flame in the lady's eye
Unseen by the courtiers standing by

Burned through his lace and titled wreath,
Burned through his body's jeweled sheath,
Till it touched the steel of the man beneath!

(And yet, mayhap, no more was meant
Than to point a well-worn compliment,
And the lady's beauty, her worst intent.)

Howbeit, the Marquis bowed again:
"Who rules with awe well serveth Spain,
But best whose law is love made plain."

Be sure that night no pillow prest
The seneschal, but with the rest
Watched, as was due a royal guest,

Watched from the wall till he saw the square
Fill with the moonlight, white and bare,
Watched till he saw two shadows fare

Out from his garden, where the shade
That the old church tower and belfry made
Like a benedictory hand was laid.

Few words spoke the seneschal as he turned

To his nearest sentry: "These monks have learned
That stolen fruit is sweetly earned.

"Myself shall punish yon acolyte
Who gathers my garden grapes by night;
Meanwhile, wait thou till the morning light."

Yet not till the sun was riding high
Did the sentry meet his commander's eye,
Nor then till the Viceroy stood by.

To the lovers of grave formalities
No greeting was ever so fine, I wis,
As this host's and guest's high courtesies!

The seneschal feared, as the wind was west,
A blast from Morena had chilled his rest;
The Viceroy languidly confest

That cares of state, and he dared to say
Some fears that the King could not repay
The thoughtful zeal of his host, some way

Had marred his rest. Yet he trusted much
None shared his wakefulness; though such
Indeed might be! If he dared to touch

A theme so fine, the bride, perchance,
Still slept! At least, they missed her glance
To give this greeting countenance.

Be sure that the seneschal, in turn,
Was deeply bowed with the grave concern
Of the painful news his guest should learn:

"Last night, to her father's dying bed
By a priest was the lady summoned;
Nor know we yet how well she sped,

"But hope for the best." The grave Viceroy
(Though grieved his visit had such alloy)
Must still wish the seneschal great joy

Of a bride so true to her filial trust!
Yet now, as the day waxed on, they must
To horse, if they'd 'scape the noonday dust.

"Nay," said the seneschal, "at least,
To mend the news of this funeral priest,
Myself shall ride as your escort east."

The Viceroy bowed. Then turned aside
To his nearest follower: "With me ride
You and Felipe on either side.

"And list! Should anything me befall,
Mischance of ambush or musket-ball,
Cleave to his saddle yon seneschal!

"No more." Then gravely in accents clear
Took formal leave of his late good cheer;
Whiles the seneschal whispered a musketeer,

Carelessly stroking his pommel top:
"If from the saddle ye see me drop,
Riddle me quickly yon solemn fop!"

So these, with many a compliment,
Each on his own dark thought intent,
With grave politeness onward went,

Riding high, and in sight of all,
Viceroy, escort, and seneschal,
Under the shade of the Almandral;

Holding their secret hard and fast,
Silent and grave they ride at last
Into the dusty traveled Past.

Even like this they passed away
Two hundred years ago to-day.
What of the lady? Who shall say?

Do the souls of the dying ever yearn
To some favored spot for the dust's return,
For the homely peace of the family urn?

I know not. Yet did the seneschal,
Chancing in after-years to fall
Pierced by a Flemish musket-ball,

Call to his side a trusty friar,
And bid him swear, as his last desire,
To bear his corse to San Pedro's choir

At Leon, where 'neath a shield azure
Should his mortal frame find sepulture:
This much, for the pains Christ did endure.

Be sure that the friar loyally
Fulfilled his trust by land and sea,
Till the spires of Leon silently

Rose through the green of the Almandral,
As if to beckon the seneschal
To his kindred dust 'neath the choir wall.

I wot that the saints on either side
Leaned from their niches open-eyed
To see the doors of the church swing wide;

That the wounds of the Saviour on either flank
Bled fresh, as the mourners, rank by rank,
Went by with the coffin, clank on clank.

For why? When they raised the marble door
Of the tomb, untouched for years before,
The friar swooned on the choir floor;

For there, in her laces and festal dress,
Lay the dead man's wife, her loveliness
Scarcely changed by her long duress,

As on the night she had passed away;
Only that near her a dagger lay,
With the written legend, "Por el Rey."

What was their greeting, the groom and bride,
They whom that steel and the years divide?
I know not. Here they lie side by side.

Side by side! Though the king has his way,
Even the dead at last have their day.
Make you the moral. "Por el Rey!"

RAMON

(REFUGIO MINE, NORTHERN MEXICO)

Drunk and senseless in his place,
Prone and sprawling on his face,
More like brute than any man
Alive or dead,
By his great pump out of gear,
Lay the peon engineer,
Waking only just to hear,
Overhead,
Angry tones that called his name,
Oaths and cries of bitter blame,
Woke to hear all this, and, waking, turned and fled!

"To the man who'll bring to me,"
Cried Intendant Harry Lee,
Harry Lee, the English foreman of the mine,
"Bring the sot alive or dead,
I will give to him," he said,
"Fifteen hundred pesos down,
Just to set the rascal's crown
Underneath this heel of mine:
Since but death
Deserves the man whose deed,
Be it vice or want of heed,
Stops the pumps that give us breath,
Stops the pumps that suck the death
From the poisoned lower levels of the mine!"

No one answered; for a cry
From the shaft rose up on high,
And shuffling, scrambling, tumbling from below,
Came the miners each, the bolder
Mounting on the weaker's shoulder,
Grappling, clinging to their hold or
Letting go,
As the weaker gasped and fell
From the ladder to the well,
To the poisoned pit of hell
Down below!

"To the man who sets them free,"
Cried the foreman, Harry Lee,
Harry Lee, the English foreman of the mine,
"Brings them out and sets them free,
I will give that man," said he,
"Twice that sum, who with a rope
Face to face with Death shall cope.
Let him come who dares to hope!"
"Hold your peace!" some one replied,
Standing by the foreman's side;
"There has one already gone, whoe'er he be!"

Then they held their breath with awe,
Pulling on the rope, and saw
Fainting figures reappear,
On the black rope swinging clear,
Fastened by some skillful hand from below;
Till a score the level gained,
And but one alone remained,
He the hero and the last,
He whose skillful hand made fast
The long line that brought them back to hope and cheer!

Haggard, gasping, down dropped he

At the feet of Harry Lee,
Harry Lee, the English foreman of the mine.
"I have come," he gasped, "to claim
Both rewards. Senor, my name
Is Ramon!
I'm the drunken engineer,
I'm the coward, Senor" Here
He fell over, by that sign,
Dead as stone!

DON DIEGO OF THE SOUTH

(REFECTORY, MISSION SAN GABRIEL, 1869)

Good! said the Padre, believe me still,
"Don Giovanni," or what you will,
The type's eternal! We knew him here
As Don Diego del Sud. I fear
The story's no new one! Will you hear?

One of those spirits you can't tell why
God has permitted. Therein I
Have the advantage, for I hold
That wolves are sent to the purest fold,
And we'd save the wolf if we'd get the lamb.
You're no believer? Good! I am.

Well, for some purpose, I grant you dim,
The Don loved women, and they loved him.
Each thought herself his LAST love! Worst,
Many believed that they were his FIRST!
And, such are these creatures since the Fall,
The very doubt had a charm for all!

You laugh! You are young, but I indeed
I have no patience... To proceed:
You saw, as you passed through the upper town,
The Eucinal where the road goes down
To San Felipe! There one morn
They found Diego, his mantle torn,
And as many holes through his doublet's band
As there were wronged husbands, you understand!

"Dying," so said the gossips. "Dead"
Was what the friars who found him said.
May be. Quien sabe? Who else should know?
It was a hundred years ago.
There was a funeral. Small indeed
Private. What would you? To proceed:

Scarcely the year had flown. One night
The Commandante awoke in fright,
Hearing below his casement's bar
The well-known twang of the Don's guitar;
And rushed to the window, just to see
His wife a-swoon on the balcony.

One week later, Don Juan Ramirez
Found his own daughter, the Dona Inez,
Pale as a ghost, leaning out to hear
The song of that phantom cavalier.
Even Alcalde Pedro Blas
Saw, it was said, through his niece's glass,
The shade of Diego twice repass.

What these gentlemen each confessed
Heaven and the Church only knows. At best
The case was a bad one. How to deal
With Sin as a Ghost, they couldn't but feel
Was an awful thing. Till a certain Fray
Humbly offered to show the way.

And the way was this. Did I say before
That the Fray was a stranger? No, Senor?
Strange! very strange! I should have said
That the very week that the Don lay dead
He came among us. Bread he broke
Silent, nor ever to one he spoke.
So he had vowed it! Below his brows
His face was hidden. There are such vows!

Strange! are they not? You do not use
Snuff? A bad habit!

Well, the views
Of the Fray were these: that the penance done
By the caballeros was right; but one
Was due from the CAUSE, and that, in brief,
Was Dona Dolores Gomez, chief,
And Inez, Sanchicha, Concepcion,
And Carmen, well, half the girls in town
On his tablets the Friar had written down.

These were to come on a certain day
And ask at the hands of the pious Fray
For absolution. That done, small fear
But the shade of Diego would disappear.

They came; each knelt in her turn and place
To the pious Fray with his hidden face

And voiceless lips, and each again
Took back her soul freed from spot or stain,
Till the Dona Inez, with eyes downcast
And a tear on their fringes, knelt her last.

And then, perhaps that her voice was low
From fear or from shame, the monks said so
But the Fray leaned forward, when, presto! all
Were thrilled by a scream, and saw her fall
Fainting beside the confessional.

And so was the ghost of Diego laid
As the Fray had said. Never more his shade
Was seen at San Gabriel's Mission. Eh!
The girl interests you? I dare say!
"Nothing," said she, when they brought her to
"Only a faintness!" They spoke more true
Who said 'twas a stubborn soul. But then
Women are women, and men are men!

So, to return. As I said before,
Having got the wolf, by the same high law
We saved the lamb in the wolf's own jaw,
And that's my moral. The tale, I fear,
But poorly told. Yet it strikes me here
Is stuff for a moral. What's your view?
You smile, Don Pancho. Ah! that's like you!

AT THE HACIENDA

Know I not whom thou mayst be
Carved upon this olive-tree,
"Manuela of La Torre,"
For around on broken walls
Summer sun and spring rain falls,
And in vain the low wind calls
"Manuela of La Torre."

Of that song no words remain
But the musical refrain,
"Manuela of La Torre."
Yet at night, when winds are still,
Tinkles on the distant hill
A guitar, and words that thrill
Tell to me the old, old story,
Old when first thy charms were sung,
Old when these old walls were young,
"Manuela of La Torre."

FRIAR PEDRO'S RIDE

It was the morning season of the year;
It was the morning era of the land;
The watercourses rang full loud and clear;
Portala's cross stood where Portala's hand
Had planted it when Faith was taught by Fear,
When monks and missions held the sole command
Of all that shore beside the peaceful sea,
Where spring-tides beat their long-drawn reveille.

Out of the mission of San Luis Rey,
All in that brisk, tumultuous spring weather,
Rode Friar Pedro, in a pious way,
With six dragoons in cuirasses of leather,
Each armed alike for either prayer or fray;
Handcuffs and missals they had slung together,
And as an aid the gospel truth to scatter
Each swung a lasso, alias a "riata."

In sooth, that year the harvest had been slack,
The crop of converts scarce worth computation;
Some souls were lost, whose owners had turned back
To save their bodies frequent flagellation;
And some preferred the songs of birds, alack!
To Latin matins and their souls' salvation,
And thought their own wild whoopings were less dreary
Than Father Pedro's droning miserere.

To bring them back to matins and to prime,
To pious works and secular submission,
To prove to them that liberty was crime,
This was, in fact, the Padre's present mission;
To get new souls perchance at the same time,
And bring them to a "sense of their condition,"
That easy phrase, which, in the past and present,
Means making that condition most unpleasant.

He saw the glebe land guiltless of a furrow;
He saw the wild oats wrestle on the hill;
He saw the gopher working in his burrow;
He saw the squirrel scampering at his will:
He saw all this, and felt no doubt a thorough
And deep conviction of God's goodness; still
He failed to see that in His glory He
Yet left the humblest of His creatures free.

He saw the flapping crow, whose frequent note
Voiced the monotony of land and sky,

Mocking with graceless wing and rusty coat
His priestly presence as he trotted by.
He would have cursed the bird by bell and rote,
But other game just then was in his eye,
A savage camp, whose occupants preferred
Their heathen darkness to the living Word.

He rang his bell, and at the martial sound
Twelve silver spurs their jingling rowels clashed;
Six horses sprang across the level ground
As six dragoons in open order dashed;
Above their heads the lassos circled round,
In every eye a pious fervor flashed;
They charged the camp, and in one moment more
They lassoed six and reconverted four.

The Friar saw the conflict from a knoll,
And sang Laus Deo and cheered on his men:
"Well thrown, Bautista, that's another soul;
After him, Gomez, try it once again;
This way, Felipe, there the heathen stole;
Bones of St. Francis! surely that makes TEN;
Te Deum laudamus but they're very wild;
Non nobis Domine, all right, my child!"

When at that moment, as the story goes
A certain squaw, who had her foes eluded,
Ran past the Friar, just before his nose.
He stared a moment, and in silence brooded;
Then in his breast a pious frenzy rose
And every other prudent thought excluded;
He caught a lasso, and dashed in a canter
After that Occidental Atalanta.

High o'er his head he swirled the dreadful noose;
But, as the practice was quite unfamiliar,
His first cast tore Felipe's captive loose,
And almost choked Tiburcio Camilla,
And might have interfered with that brave youth's
Ability to gorge the tough tortilla;
But all things come by practice, and at last
His flying slip-knot caught the maiden fast.

Then rose above the plain a mingled yell
Of rage and triumph, a demoniac whoop:
The Padre heard it like a passing knell,
And would have loosened his unchristian loop;
But the tough raw-hide held the captive well,
And held, alas! too well the captor-dupe;
For with one bound the savage fled amain,
Dragging horse, Friar, down the lonely plain.

Down the arroyo, out across the mead,
By heath and hollow, sped the flying maid,
Dragging behind her still the panting steed
And helpless Friar, who in vain essayed
To cut the lasso or to check his speed.
He felt himself beyond all human aid,
And trusted to the saints, and, for that matter,
To some weak spot in Felipe's riata.

Alas! the lasso had been duly blessed,
And, like baptism, held the flying wretch,
A doctrine that the priest had oft expressed,
Which, like the lasso, might be made to stretch,
But would not break; so neither could divest
Themselves of it, but, like some awful fetch,
The holy Friar had to recognize
The image of his fate in heathen guise.

He saw the glebe land guiltless of a furrow;
He saw the wild oats wrestle on the hill;
He saw the gopher standing in his burrow;
He saw the squirrel scampering at his will:
He saw all this, and felt no doubt how thorough
The contrast was to his condition; still
The squaw kept onward to the sea, till night
And the cold sea-fog hid them both from sight.

The morning came above the serried coast,
Lighting the snow-peaks with its beacon-fires,
Driving before it all the fleet-winged host
Of chattering birds above the Mission spires,
Filling the land with light and joy, but most
The savage woods with all their leafy lyres;
In pearly tints and opal flame and fire
The morning came, but not the holy Friar.

Weeks passed away. In vain the Fathers sought
Some trace or token that might tell his story;
Some thought him dead, or, like Elijah, caught
Up to the heavens in a blaze of glory.
In this surmise some miracles were wrought
On his account, and souls in purgatory
Were thought to profit from his intercession;
In brief, his absence made a "deep impression."

A twelvemonth passed; the welcome Spring once more
Made green the hills beside the white-faced Mission,
Spread her bright dais by the western shore,
And sat enthroned, a most resplendent vision.
The heathen converts thronged the chapel door

At morning mass, when, says the old tradition,
A frightful whoop throughout the church resounded,
And to their feet the congregation bounded.

A tramp of hoofs upon the beaten course,
Then came a sight that made the bravest quail:
A phantom Friar on a spectre horse,
Dragged by a creature decked with horns and tail.
By the lone Mission, with the whirlwind's force,
They madly swept, and left a sulphurous trail:
And that was all, enough to tell the story,
And leave unblessed those souls in purgatory.

And ever after, on that fatal day
That Friar Pedro rode abroad lassoing,
A ghostly couple came and went away
With savage whoop and heathenish hallooing,
Which brought discredit on San Luis Rey,
And proved the Mission's ruin and undoing;
For ere ten years had passed, the squaw and Friar
Performed to empty walls and fallen spire.

The Mission is no more; upon its wall.
The golden lizards slip, or breathless pause,
Still as the sunshine brokenly that falls
Through crannied roof and spider-webs of gauze;
No more the bell its solemn warning calls,
A holier silence thrills and overawes;
And the sharp lights and shadows of to-day
Outline the Mission of San Luis Rey.

IN THE MISSION GARDEN

(1865)

FATHER FELIPE

I speak not the English well, but Pachita,
She speak for me; is it not so, my Pancha?
Eh, little rogue? Come, salute me the stranger
Americano.

Sir, in my country we say, "Where the heart is,
There live the speech." Ah! you not understand? So!
Pardon an old man, what you call "old fogy,"
Padre Felipe!

Old, Senor, old! just so old as the Mission.
You see that pear-tree? How old you think, Senor?

Fifteen year? Twenty? Ah, Senor, just fifty
Gone since I plant him!

You like the wine? It is some at the Mission,
Made from the grape of the year eighteen hundred;
All the same time when the earthquake he come to
San Juan Bautista.

But Pancha is twelve, and she is the rose-tree;
And I am the olive, and this is the garden:
And "Pancha" we say, but her name is "Francisca,"
Same like her mother.

Eh, you knew HER? No? Ah! it is a story;
But I speak not, like Pachita, the English:
So! if I try, you will sit here beside me,
And shall not laugh, eh?

When the American come to the Mission,
Many arrive at the house of Francisca:
One, he was fine man, he buy the cattle
Of Jose Castro.

So! he came much, and Francisca, she saw him:
And it was love, and a very dry season;
And the pears bake on the tree, and the rain come,
But not Francisca.

Not for one year; and one night I have walk much
Under the olive-tree, when comes Francisca,
Comes to me here, with her child, this Francisca,
Under the olive-tree.

Sir, it was sad;... but I speak not the English;
So!... she stay here, and she wait for her husband:
He come no more, and she sleep on the hillside;
There stands Pachita.

Ah! there's the Angelus. Will you not enter?
Or shall you walk in the garden with Pancha?
Go, little rogue-st! attend to the stranger!
Adios, Senor.

PACHITA (briskly).

So, he's been telling that yarn about mother!
Bless you! he tells it to every stranger:
Folks about yer say the old man's my father;
What's your opinion?

THE LOST GALLEON*

In sixteen hundred and forty-one,
The regular yearly galleon,
Laden with odorous gums and spice,
India cottons and India rice,
And the richest silks of far Cathay,
Was due at Acapulco Bay.

Due she was, and overdue,
Galleon, merchandise and crew,
Creeping along through rain and shine,
Through the tropics, under the line.
The trains were waiting outside the walls,
The wives of sailors thronged the town,
The traders sat by their empty stalls,
And the Viceroy himself came down;
The bells in the tower were all a-trip,
Te Deums were on each Father's lip,
The limes were ripening in the sun
For the sick of the coming galleon.

All in vain. Weeks passed away,
And yet no galleon saw the bay.
India goods advanced in price;
The Governor missed his favorite spice;
The Senoritas mourned for sandal
And the famous cottons of Coromandel;
And some for an absent lover lost,
And one for a husband, Dona Julia,
Wife of the captain tempest-tossed,
In circumstances so peculiar;
Even the Fathers, unawares,
Grumbled a little at their prayers;
And all along the coast that year
Votive candles wore scarce and dear.

Never a tear bedims the eye
That time and patience will not dry;
Never a lip is curved with pain
That can't be kissed into smiles again;
And these same truths, as far as I know,
Obtained on the coast of Mexico
More than two hundred years ago,
In sixteen hundred and fifty-one,
Ten years after the deed was done,
And folks had forgotten the galleon:
The divers plunged in the gulf for pearls,
White as the teeth of the Indian girls;
The traders sat by their full bazaars;

The mules with many a weary load,
And oxen dragging their creaking cars,
Came and went on the mountain road.

Where was the galleon all this while?
Wrecked on some lonely coral isle,
Burnt by the roving sea-marauders,
Or sailing north under secret orders?
Had she found the Anian passage famed,
By lying Maldonado claimed,
And sailed through the sixty-fifth degree
Direct to the North Atlantic Sea?
Or had she found the "River of Kings,"
Of which De Fonte told such strange things,
In sixteen forty? Never a sign,
East or west or under the line,
They saw of the missing galleon;
Never a sail or plank or chip
They found of the long-lost treasure-ship,
Or enough to build a tale upon.
But when she was lost, and where and how,
Are the facts we're coming to just now.

Take, if you please, the chart of that day,
Published at Madrid, por el Rey;
Look for a spot in the old South Sea,
The hundred and eightieth degree
Longitude west of Madrid: there,
Under the equatorial glare,
Just where the east and west are one,
You'll find the missing galleon,
You'll find the San Gregorio, yet
Riding the seas, with sails all set,
Fresh as upon the very day
She sailed from Acapulco Bay.

How did she get there? What strange spell
Kept her two hundred years so well,
Free from decay and mortal taint?
What but the prayers of a patron saint!

A hundred leagues from Manilla town,
The San Gregorio's helm came down;
Round she went on her heel, and not
A cable's length from a galliot
That rocked on the waters just abreast
Of the galleon's course, which was west-sou'-west.

Then said the galleon's commandante,
General Pedro Sobriente
(That was his rank on land and main,

A regular custom of Old Spain),
"My pilot is dead of scurvy: may
I ask the longitude, time, and day?"
The first two given and compared;
The third, the commandante stared!
"The FIRST of June? I make it second."
Said the stranger, "Then you've wrongly reckoned;
I make it FIRST: as you came this way,
You should have lost, d'ye see, a day;
Lost a day, as plainly see,
On the hundred and eightieth degree."
"Lost a day?" "Yes; if not rude,
When did you make east longitude?"
"On the ninth of May, our patron's day."
"On the ninth? YOU HAD NO NINTH OF MAY!
Eighth and tenth was there; but stay"
Too late; for the galleon bore away.

Lost was the day they should have kept,
Lost unheeded and lost unwept;
Lost in a way that made search vain,
Lost in a trackless and boundless main;
Lost like the day of Job's awful curse,
In his third chapter, third and fourth verse;
Wrecked was their patron's only day,
What would the holy Fathers say?

Said the Fray Antonio Estavan,
The galleon's chaplain, a learned man,
"Nothing is lost that you can regain;
And the way to look for a thing is plain,
To go where you lost it, back again.
Back with your galleon till you see
The hundred and eightieth degree.
Wait till the rolling year goes round,
And there will the missing day be found;
For you'll find, if computation's true,
That sailing EAST will give to you
Not only one ninth of May, but two,
One for the good saint's present cheer,
And one for the day we lost last year."

Back to the spot sailed the galleon;
Where, for a twelvemonth, off and on
The hundred and eightieth degree
She rose and fell on a tropic sea.
But lo! when it came to the ninth of May,
All of a sudden becalmed she lay
One degree from that fatal spot,
Without the power to move a knot;
And of course the moment she lost her way,

Gone was her chance to save that day.

To cut a lengthening story short,
She never saved it. Made the sport
Of evil spirits and baffling wind,
She was always before or just behind,
One day too soon or one day too late,
And the sun, meanwhile, would never wait.
She had two Eighths, as she idly lay,
Two Tenths, but never a NINTH of May;
And there she rides through two hundred years
Of dreary penance and anxious fears;
Yet, through the grace of the saint she served,
Captain and crew are still preserved.

By a computation that still holds good,
Made by the Holy Brotherhood,
The San Gregorio will cross that line
In nineteen hundred and thirty-nine:
Just three hundred years to a day
From the time she lost the ninth of May.
And the folk in Acapulco town,
Over the waters looking down,
Will see in the glow of the setting sun
The sails of the missing galleon,
And the royal standard of Philip Rey,
The gleaming mast and glistening spar,
As she nears the surf of the outer bar.
A Te Deum sung on her crowded deck,
An odor of spice along the shore,
A crash, a cry from a shattered wreck,
And the yearly galleon sails no more
In or out of the olden bay;
For the blessed patron has found his day.

Such is the legend. Hear this truth:
Over the trackless past, somewhere,
Lie the lost days of our tropic youth,
Only regained by faith and prayer,
Only recalled by prayer and plaint:
Each lost day has its patron saint!

See note 1

III. IN DIALECT

"JIM"

Say there! P'r'aps

Some on you chaps
Might know Jim Wild?
Well, no offense:
Thar ain't no sense
In gittin' riled!

Jim was my chum
Up on the Bar:
That's why I come
Down from up yar,
Lookin' for Jim.
Thank ye, sir! YOU
Ain't of that crew,
Blest if you are!

Money? Not much:
That ain't my kind;
I ain't no such.
Rum? I don't mind,
Seein' it's you.

Well, this yer Jim,
Did you know him?
Jes' 'bout your size;
Same kind of eyes;
Well, that is strange:
Why, it's two year
Since he came here,
Sick, for a change.

Well, here's to us:
Eh?
The hell you say!
Dead?
That little cuss?

What makes you star',
You over thar?
Can't a man drop
's glass in yer shop
But you must r'ar?
It wouldn't take
Damned much to break
You and your bar.

Dead!
Poor-little-Jim!
Why, thar was me,
Jones, and Bob Lee,
Harry and Ben,
No-account men:

Then to take HIM!

Well, thar - Good-by
No more, sir - I
Eh?
What's that you say?
Why, dern it! sho!
No? Yes! By Joe!
Sold!

Sold! Why, you limb,
You ornery,
Derned old
Long-legged Jim.

CHIQUITA

Beautiful! Sir, you may say so. Thar isn't her match in the county;
Is thar, old gal, Chiquita, my darling, my beauty?
Feel of that neck, sir, thar's velvet! Whoa! steady, ah, will you, you vixen!
Whoa! I say. Jack, trot her out; let the gentleman look at her paces.

Morgan! she ain't nothing else, and I've got the papers to prove it.
Sired by Chippewa Chief, and twelve hundred dollars won't buy her.
Briggs of Tuolumne owned her. Did you know Briggs of Tuolumne?
Busted hisself in White Pine, and blew out his brains down in 'Frisco?

Hedn't no savey, hed Briggs. Thar, Jack! that'll do, quit that foolin'!
Nothin' to what she kin do, when she's got her work cut out before her.
Hosses is hosses, you know, and likewise, too, jockeys is jockeys:
And 'tain't ev'ry man as can ride as knows what a hoss has got in him.

Know the old ford on the Fork, that nearly got Flanigan's leaders?
Nasty in daylight, you bet, and a mighty rough ford in low water!
Well, it ain't six weeks ago that me and the Jedge and his nevey
Struck for that ford in the night, in the rain, and the water all round us;

Up to our flanks in the gulch, and Rattlesnake Creek just a-bilin',
Not a plank left in the dam, and nary a bridge on the river.
I had the gray, and the Jedge had his roan, and his nevey, Chiquita;
And after us trundled the rocks jest loosed from the top of the canyon.

Lickity, lickity, switch, we came to the ford, and Chiquita
Buckled right down to her work, and, a fore I could yell to her rider,
Took water jest at the ford, and there was the Jedge and me standing,
And twelve hundred dollars of hoss-flesh afloat, and a-driftin' to thunder!

Would ye b'lieve it? That night, that hoss, that 'ar filly, Chiquita,
Walked herself into her stall, and stood there, all quiet and dripping:

Clean as a beaver or rat, with nary a buckle of harness,
Just as she swam the Fork, that hoss, that 'ar filly, Chiquita.

That's what I call a hoss! And - What did you say? Oh, the nevey?
Drownded, I reckon, leastways, he never kem beck to deny it.
Ye see the derned fool had no seat, ye couldn't have made him a rider;
And then, ye know, boys will be boys, and hosses, well, hosses is hosses!

DOW'S FLAT

(1856)

Dow's Flat. That's its name;
And I reckon that you
Are a stranger? The same?
Well, I thought it was true,
For thar isn't a man on the river as can't spot the place at first view.

It was called after Dow,
Which the same was an ass,
And as to the how
Thet the thing kem to pass,
Jest tie up your hoss to that buckeye, and sit ye down here in the grass.

You see this 'yer Dow
Hed the worst kind of luck;
He slipped up somehow
On each thing thet he struck.
Why, ef he'd a straddled thet fence-rail, the derned thing'd get up and buck.

He mined on the bar
Till he couldn't pay rates;
He was smashed by a car
When he tunneled with Bates;
And right on the top of his trouble kem his wife and five kids from the States.

It was rough, mighty rough;
But the boys they stood by,
And they brought him the stuff
For a house, on the sly;
And the old woman, well, she did washing, and took on when no one was nigh.

But this 'yer luck of Dow's
Was so powerful mean
That the spring near his house
Dried right up on the green;
And he sunk forty feet down for water, but nary a drop to be seen.

Then the bar petered out,

And the boys wouldn't stay;
And the chills got about,
And his wife fell away;
But Dow in his well kept a peggin' in his usual ridikilous way.

One day, it was June,
And a year ago, jest
This Dow kem at noon
To his work like the rest,
With a shovel and pick on his shoulder, and derringer hid in his breast.

He goes to the well,
And he stands on the brink,
And stops for a spell
Jest to listen and think:
For the sun in his eyes (jest like this, sir!), you see, kinder made the cuss blink.

His two ragged gals
In the gulch were at play,
And a gownd that was Sal's
Kinder flapped on a bay:
Not much for a man to be leavin', but his all, as I've heer'd the folks say.

And - That's a peart hoss
Thet you've got, ain't it now?
What might be her cost?
Eh? Oh! Well, then, Dow
Let's see, well, that forty-foot grave wasn't his, sir, that day, anyhow.

For a blow of his pick
Sorter caved in the side,
And he looked and turned sick,
Then he trembled and cried.
For you see the dern cuss had struck - "Water?" - Beg your parding, young man, there you lied!

It was GOLD, in the quartz,
And it ran all alike;
And I reckon five oughts
Was the worth of that strike;
And that house with the coopilow's his'n, which the same isn't bad for a Pike.

Thet's why it's Dow's Flat;
And the thing of it is
That he kinder got that
Through sheer contrairiness:
For 'twas WATER the derned cuss was seekin', and his luck made him certain to miss.

Thet's so! Thar's your way,
To the left of yon tree;
But-a-look h'yur, say?
Won't you come up to tea?

No? Well, then the next time you're passin'; and ask after Dow, and thet's ME.

IN THE TUNNEL

Didn't know Flynn,
Flynn of Virginia,
Long as he's been 'yar?
Look 'ee here, stranger,
Whar HEV you been?

Here in this tunnel
He was my pardner,
That same Tom Flynn,
Working together,
In wind and weather,
Day out and in.

Didn't know Flynn!
Well, that IS queer;
Why, it's a sin
To think of Tom Flynn,
Tom with his cheer,
Tom without fear,
Stranger, look 'yar!

Thar in the drift,
Back to the wall,
He held the timbers
Ready to fall;
Then in the darkness
I heard him call:
"Run for your life, Jake!
Run for your wife's sake!
Don't wait for me."
And that was all
Heard in the din,
Heard of Tom Flynn,
Flynn of Virginia.

That's all about
Flynn of Virginia.
That lets me out.
Here in the damp,
Out of the sun,
That 'ar derned lamp
Makes my eyes run.
Well, there, I'm done!

But, sir, when you'll

Hear the next fool
Asking of Flynn,
Flynn of Virginia,
Just you chip in,
Say you knew Flynn;
Say that you've been 'yar.

"CICELY"

(ALKALI STATION)

Cicely says you're a poet; maybe, I ain't much on rhyme:
I reckon you'd give me a hundred, and beat me every time.
Poetry! that's the way some chaps puts up an idee,
But I takes mine "straight without sugar," and that's what's the
matter with me.

Poetry! just look round you, alkali, rock, and sage;
Sage-brush, rock, and alkali; ain't it a pretty page!
Sun in the east at mornin', sun in the west at night,
And the shadow of this 'yer station the on'y thing moves in sight.

Poetry! Well now Polly! Polly, run to your mam;
Run right away, my pooty! By-by! Ain't she a lamb?
Poetry! that reminds me o' suthin' right in that suit:
Jest shet that door thar, will yer? for Cicely's ears is cute.

Ye noticed Polly, the baby? A month afore she was born,
Cicely, my old woman, was moody-like and forlorn;
Out of her head and crazy, and talked of flowers and trees;
Family man yourself, sir? Well, you know what a woman be's.

Narvous she was, and restless, said that she "couldn't stay."
Stay! and the nearest woman seventeen miles away.
But I fixed it up with the doctor, and he said he be on hand,
And I kinder stuck by the shanty, and fenced in that bit o' land.

One night, the tenth of October, I woke with a chill and a fright,
For the door it was standing open, and Cicely warn't in sight,
But a note was pinned on the blanket, which it said that she "couldn't stay,"
But had gone to visit her neighbor, seventeen miles away!

When and how she stampeded, I didn't wait for to see,
For out in the road, next minit, I started as wild as she;
Running first this way and that way, like a hound that is off the scent,
For there warn't no track in the darkness to tell me the way she went.

I've had some mighty mean moments afore I kem to this spot,
Lost on the Plains in '50, drownded almost and shot;

But out on this alkali desert, a-hunting a crazy wife,
Was ra'ly as on-satis-factory as anything in my life.

"Cicely! Cicely! Cicely!" I called, and I held my breath,
And "Cicely!" came from the canyon, and all was as still as death.
And "Cicely! Cicely! Cicely!" came from the rocks below,
And jest but a whisper of "Cicely!" down from them peaks of snow.

I ain't what you call religious, but I jest looked up to the sky,
And this 'yer's to what I'm coming, and maybe ye think I lie:
But up away to the east'ard, yaller and big and far,
I saw of a suddent rising the singlerist kind of star.

Big and yaller and dancing, it seemed to beckon to me:
Yaller and big and dancing, such as you never see:
Big and yaller and dancing, I never saw such a star,
And I thought of them sharps in the Bible, and I went for it then and thar.

Over the brush and bowlders I stumbled and pushed ahead,
Keeping the star afore me, I went wherever it led.
It might hev been for an hour, when suddent and peart and nigh,
Out of the yearth afore me thar riz up a baby's cry.

Listen! thar's the same music; but her lungs they are stronger now
Than the day I packed her and her mother, I'm derned if I jest know how.
But the doctor kem the next minit, and the joke o' the whole thing is
That Cis never knew what happened from that very night to this!

But Cicely says you're a poet, and maybe you might, some day,
Jest sling her a rhyme 'bout a baby that was born in a curious way,
And see what she says; and, old fellow, when you speak of the star,
don't tell
As how 'twas the doctor's lantern, for maybe 'twon't sound so well.

PENELOPE

(SIMPSON'S BAR, 1858)

So you've kem 'yer agen,
And one answer won't do?
Well, of all the derned men
That I've struck, it is you.
O Sal! 'yer's that derned fool from Simpson's, cavortin' round 'yer in the dew.

Kem in, ef you WILL.
Thar, quit! Take a cheer.
Not that; you can't fill
Them theer cushings this year,
For that cheer was my old man's, Joe Simpson, and they don't make such men about 'yer.

He was tall, was my Jack,
And as strong as a tree.
Thar's his gun on the rack,
Jest you heft it, and see.
And YOU come a courtin' his widder! Lord! where can that critter, Sal, be!

You'd fill my Jack's place?
And a man of your size,
With no baird to his face,
Nor a snap to his eyes,
And nary - Sho! thar! I was foolin', I was, Joe, for sartain, don't rise.

Sit down. Law! why, sho!
I'm as weak as a gal.
Sal! Don't you go, Joe,
Or I'll faint, sure, I shall.
Sit down, ANYWHEER, where you like, Joe, in that cheer, if you choose, Lord! where's Sal?

PLAIN LANGUAGE FROM TRUTHFUL JAMES

(TABLE MOUNTAIN, 1870)

Which I wish to remark,
And my language is plain,
That for ways that are dark
And for tricks that are vain,
The heathen Chinee is peculiar,
Which the same I would rise to explain.

Ah Sin was his name;
And I shall not deny,
In regard to the same,
What that name might imply;
But his smile it was pensive and childlike,
As I frequent remarked to Bill Nye.

It was August the third,
And quite soft was the skies;
Which it might be inferred
That Ah Sin was likewise;
Yet he played it that day upon William
And me in a way I despise.

Which we had a small game,
And Ah Sin took a hand:
It was Euchre. The same
He did not understand;
But he smiled as he sat by the table,

With the smile that was childlike and bland.

Yet the cards they were stocked
In a way that I grieve,
And my feelings were shocked
At the state of Nye's sleeve,
Which was stuffed full of aces and bowers,
And the same with intent to deceive.

But the hands that were played
By that heathen Chinee,
And the points that he made,
Were quite frightful to see,
Till at last he put down a right bower,
Which the same Nye had dealt unto me.

Then I looked up at Nye,
And he gazed upon me;
And he rose with a sigh,
And said, "Can this be?
We are ruined by Chinese cheap labor,"
And he went for that heathen Chinee.

In the scene that ensued
I did not take a hand,
But the floor it was strewed
Like the leaves on the strand
With the cards that Ah Sin had been hiding,
In the game "he did not understand."

In his sleeves, which were long,
He had twenty-four packs,
Which was coming it strong,
Yet I state but the facts;
And we found on his nails, which were taper,
What is frequent in tapers, that's wax.

Which is why I remark,
And my language is plain,
That for ways that are dark
And for tricks that are vain,
The heathen Chinee is peculiar,
Which the same I am free to maintain.

THE SOCIETY UPON THE STANISLAUS

I reside at Table Mountain, and my name is Truthful James;
I am not up to small deceit or any sinful games;
And I'll tell in simple language what I know about the row

That broke up our Society upon the Stanislow.

But first I would remark, that it is not a proper plan
For any scientific gent to whale his fellow-man,
And, if a member don't agree with his peculiar whim,
To lay for that same member for to "put a head" on him.

Now nothing could be finer or more beautiful to see
Than the first six months' proceedings of that same Society,
Till Brown of Calaveras brought a lot of fossil bones
That he found within a tunnel near the tenement of Jones.

Then Brown he read a paper, and he reconstructed there,
From those same bones, an animal that was extremely rare;
And Jones then asked the Chair for a suspension of the rules,
Till he could prove that those same bones was one of his lost mules.

Then Brown he smiled a bitter smile, and said he was at fault,
It seemed he had been trespassing on Jones's family vault;
He was a most sarcastic man, this quiet Mr. Brown,
And on several occasions he had cleaned out the town.

Now I hold it is not decent for a scientific gent
To say another is an ass, at least, to all intent;
Nor should the individual who happens to be meant
Reply by heaving rocks at him, to any great extent.

Then Abner Dean of Angel's raised a point of order, when
A chunk of old red sandstone took him in the abdomen,
And he smiled a kind of sickly smile, and curled up on the floor,
And the subsequent proceedings interested him no more.

For, in less time than I write it, every member did engage
In a warfare with the remnants of a palaeozoic age;
And the way they heaved those fossils in their anger was a sin,
Till the skull of an old mammoth caved the head of Thompson in.

And this is all I have to say of these improper games,
For I live at Table Mountain, and my name is Truthful James;
And I've told in simple language what I know about the row
That broke up our Society upon the Stanislow.

LUKE

(IN THE COLORADO PARK, 1873)

Wot's that you're readin'? a novel? A novel! well, darn my skin!
You a man grown and bearded and histin' such stuff ez that in
Stuff about gals and their sweethearts! No wonder you're thin ez a knife.

Look at me, clar two hundred, and never read one in my life!

That's my opinion o' novels. And ez to their lyin' round here,
They belong to the Jedge's daughter, the Jedge who came up last year
On account of his lungs and the mountains and the balsam o' pine and fir;
And his daughter, well, she read novels, and that's what's the matter with her.

Yet she was sweet on the Jedge, and stuck by him day and night,
Alone in the cabin up 'yer, till she grew like a ghost, all white.
She wus only a slip of a thing, ez light and ez up and away
Ez rifle smoke blown through the woods, but she wasn't my kind—no way!

Speakin' o' gals, d'ye mind that house ez you rise the hill,
A mile and a half from White's, and jist above Mattingly's mill?
You do? Well now THAR's a gal! What! you saw her? Oh, come now, thar! quit!
She was only bedevlin' you boys, for to me she don't cotton one bit.

Now she's what I call a gal, ez pretty and plump ez a quail;
Teeth ez white ez a hound's, and they'd go through a ten-penny nail;
Eyes that kin snap like a cap. So she asked to know "whar I was hid?"
She did! Oh, it's jist like her sass, for she's peart ez a Katydid.

But what was I talking of? Oh! the Jedge and his daughter, she read
Novels the whole day long, and I reckon she read them abed;
And sometimes she read them out loud to the Jedge on the porch where he sat,
And 'twas how "Lord Augustus" said this, and how "Lady Blanche" she said that.

But the sickest of all that I heerd was a yarn thet they read 'bout a chap,
"Leather-stocking" by name, and a hunter chock full o' the greenest o' sap;
And they asked me to hear, but I says, "Miss Mabel, not any for me;
When I likes I kin sling my own lies, and thet chap and I shouldn't agree."

Yet somehow or other that gal allus said that I brought her to mind
Of folks about whom she had read, or suthin belike of thet kind,
And thar warn't no end o' the names that she give me thet summer up here
"Robin Hood," "Leather-stocking" "Rob Roy," Oh, I tell you, the critter was queer!

And yet, ef she hadn't been spiled, she was harmless enough in her way;
She could jabber in French to her dad, and they said that she knew how to play;
And she worked me that shot-pouch up thar, which the man doesn't live ez kin use;
And slippers, you see 'em down 'yer, ez would cradle an Injin's papoose.

Yet along o' them novels, you see, she was wastin' and mopin' away,
And then she got shy with her tongue, and at last she had nothin' to say;
And whenever I happened around, her face it was hid by a book,
And it warn't till the day she left that she give me ez much ez a look.

And this was the way it was. It was night when I kem up here
To say to 'em all "good-by," for I reckoned to go for deer
At "sun up" the day they left. So I shook 'em all round by the hand,
'Cept Mabel, and she was sick, ez they give me to understand.

But jist ez I passed the house next morning at dawn, some one,
Like a little waver o' mist got up on the hill with the sun;
Miss Mabel it was, alone, all wrapped in a mantle o' lace
And she stood there straight in the road, with a touch o' the sun in her face.

And she looked me right in the eye, I'd seen suthin' like it before
When I hunted a wounded doe to the edge o' the Clear Lake Shore,
And I had my knee on its neck, and I jist was raisin' my knife,
When it give me a look like that, and well, it got off with its life.

"We are going to-day," she said, "and I thought I would say good-by
To you in your own house, Luke, these woods and the bright blue sky!
You've always been kind to us, Luke, and papa has found you still
As good as the air he breathes, and wholesome as Laurel Tree Hill.

"And we'll always think of you, Luke, as the thing we could not take away,
The balsam that dwells in the woods, the rainbow that lives in the spray.
And you'll sometimes think of ME, Luke, as you know you once used to say,
A rifle smoke blown through the woods, a moment, but never to stay."

And then we shook hands. She turned, but a-suddent she tottered and fell,
And I caught her sharp by the waist, and held her a minit. Well,
It was only a minit, you know, thet ez cold and ez white she lay
Ez a snowflake here on my breast, and then, well, she melted away

And was gone.... And thar are her books; but I says not any for me;
Good enough may be for some, but them and I mightn't agree.
They spiled a decent gal ez might hev made some chap a wife,
And look at me! clar two hundred and never read one in my life!

"THE BABES IN THE WOODS"

(BIG PINE FLAT, 1871)

"Something characteristic," eh?
Humph! I reckon you mean by that
Something that happened in our way,
Here at the crossin' of Big Pine Flat.
Times aren't now as they used to be,
When gold was flush and the boys were frisky,
And a man would pull out his battery
For anything, maybe the price of whiskey.

Nothing of that sort, eh? That's strange!
Why, I thought you might be diverted
Hearing how Jones of Red Rock Range
Drawed his "hint to the unconverted,"
And saying, "Whar will you have it?" shot

Cherokee Bob at the last debating!
What was the question I forgot,
But Jones didn't like Bob's way of stating.

Nothing of that kind, eh? You mean
Something milder? Let's see! O Joe!
Tell to the stranger that little scene
Out of the "Babes in the Woods." You know,
"Babes" was the name that we gave 'em, sir,
Two lean lads in their teens, and greener
Than even the belt of spruce and fir
Where they built their nest, and each day grew leaner.

No one knew where they came from. None
Cared to ask if they had a mother.
Runaway schoolboys, maybe. One
Tall and dark as a spruce; the other
Blue and gold in the eyes and hair,
Soft and low in his speech, but rarely
Talking with us; and we didn't care
To get at their secret at all unfairly.

For they were so quiet, so sad and shy,
Content to trust each other solely,
That somehow we'd always shut one eye,
And never seem to observe them wholly
As they passed to their work. 'Twas a worn-out claim,
And it paid them grub. They could live without it,
For the boys had a way of leaving game
In their tent, and forgetting all about it.

Yet no one asked for their secret. Dumb
It lay in their big eyes' heavy hollows.
It was understood that no one should come
To their tent unawares, save the bees and swallows.
So they lived alone. Until one warm night
I was sitting here at the tent-door, so, sir!
When out of the sunset's rosy light
Up rose the Sheriff of Mariposa.

I knew at once there was something wrong,
For his hand and his voice shook just a little,
And there isn't much you can fetch along
To make the sinews of Jack Hill brittle.
"Go warn the Babes!" he whispered, hoarse;
"Tell them I'm coming to get and scurry;
For I've got a story that's bad, and worse,
I've got a warrant: God damn it, hurry!"

Too late! they had seen him cross the hill;
I ran to their tent and found them lying

Dead in each other's arms, and still
Clasping the drug they had taken flying.
And there lay their secret cold and bare,
Their life, their trial, the old, old story!
For the sweet blue eyes and the golden hair
Was a WOMAN'S shame and a WOMAN'S glory.

"Who were they?" Ask no more, or ask
The sun that visits their grave so lightly;
Ask of the whispering reeds, or task
The mourning crickets that chirrup nightly.
All of their life but its love forgot,
Everything tender and soft and mystic,
These are our Babes in the Woods, you've got,
Well, human nature, that's characteristic.

THE LATEST CHINESE OUTRAGE

It was noon by the sun; we had finished our game,
And was passin' remarks goin' back to our claim;
Jones was countin' his chips, Smith relievin' his mind
Of ideas that a "straight" should beat "three of a kind,"
When Johnson of Elko came gallopin' down,
With a look on his face 'twixt a grin and a frown,
And he calls, "Drop your shovels and face right about,
For them Chinees from Murphy's are cleanin' us out
With their ching-a-ring-chow
And their chic-colorow
They're bent upon making
No slouch of a row."

Then Jones, my own pardner, looks up with a sigh;
"It's your wash-bill," sez he, and I answers, "You lie!"
But afore he could draw or the others could arm,
Up tumbles the Bates boys, who heard the alarm.
And a yell from the hill-top and roar of a gong,
Mixed up with remarks like "Hi! yi! Chang-a-wong,"
And bombs, shells, and crackers, that crashed through the trees,
Revealed in their war-togs four hundred Chinees!
Four hundred Chinee;
We are eight, don't ye see!
That made a square fifty
To just one o' we.

They were dressed in their best, but I grieve that that same
Was largely made up of our own, to their shame;
And my pardner's best shirt and his trousers were hung
On a spear, and above him were tauntingly swung;
While that beggar, Chey Lee, like a conjurer sat

Pullin' out eggs and chickens from Johnson's best hat;
And Bates's game rooster was part of their "loot,"
And all of Smith's pigs were skyugled to boot;
But the climax was reached and I like to have died
When my demijohn, empty, came down the hillside,
Down the hillside
What once held the pride
Of Robertson County
Pitched down the hillside!

Then we axed for a parley. When out of the din
To the front comes a-rockin' that heathen, Ah Sin!
"You owe flowty dollee, me washee you camp,
You catchee my washee, me catchee no stamp;
One dollar hap dozen, me no catchee yet,
Now that flowty dollee, no hab? how can get?
Me catchee you piggee, me sellee for cash,
It catchee me licee, you catchee no 'hash;'
Me belly good Sheliff, me lebbee when can,
Me allee same halp pin as Melican man!
But Melican man
He washee him pan
On BOTTOM side hillee
And catchee, how can?"

"Are we men?" says Joe Johnson, "and list to this jaw,
Without process of warrant or color of law?
Are we men or a-chew!" here be gasped in his speech,
For a stink-pot had fallen just out of his reach.
"Shall we stand here as idle, and let Asia pour
Her barbaric hordes on this civilized shore?
Has the White Man no country? Are we left in the lurch?
And likewise what's gone of the Established Church?
One man to four hundred is great odds, I own,
But this 'yer's a White Man, I plays it alone!"
And he sprang up the hillside, to stop him none dare
Till a yell from the top told a "White Man was there!"
A White Man was there!
We prayed he might spare
Those misguided heathens
The few clothes they wear.

They fled, and he followed, but no matter where;
They fled to escape him, the "White Man was there,"
Till we missed first his voice on the pine-wooded slope,
And we knew for the heathen henceforth was no hope;
And the yells they grew fainter, when Petersen said,
"It simply was human to bury his dead."
And then, with slow tread,
We crept up, in dread,
But found nary mortal there,

Living or dead.

But there was his trail, and the way that they came,
And yonder, no doubt, he was bagging his game.
When Jones drops his pickaxe, and Thompson says "Shoo!"
And both of 'em points to a cage of bamboo
Hanging down from a tree, with a label that swung
Conspicuous, with letters in some foreign tongue,
Which, when freely translated, the same did appear
Was the Chinese for saying, "A White Man is here!"
And as we drew near,
In anger and fear,
Bound hand and foot, Johnson
Looked down with a leer!

In his mouth was an opium pipe, which was why
He leered at us so with a drunken-like eye!
They had shaved off his eyebrows, and tacked on a cue,
They had painted his face of a coppery hue,
And rigged him all up in a heathenish suit,
Then softly departed, each man with his "loot."
Yes, every galoot,
And Ah Sin, to boot,
Had left him there hanging
Like ripening fruit.

At a mass meeting held up at Murphy's next day
There were seventeen speakers and each had his say;
There were twelve resolutions that instantly passed,
And each resolution was worse than the last;
There were fourteen petitions, which, granting the same,
Will determine what Governor Murphy's shall name;
And the man from our district that goes up next year
Goes up on one issue, that's patent and clear:
"Can the work of a mean,
Degraded, unclean
Believer in Buddha
Be held as a lien?"

TRUTHFUL JAMES TO THE EDITOR

(YREKA, 1873)

Which it is not my style
To produce needless pain
By statements that rile
Or that go 'gin the grain,
But here's Captain Jack still a-livin', and Nye has no skelp on his
brain!

On that Caucasian head
There is no crown of hair;
It has gone, it has fled!
And Echo sez "Where?"
And I asks, "Is this Nation a White Man's, and is generally things
on the square?"

She was known in the camp
As "Nye's other squaw,"
And folks of that stamp
Hez no rights in the law,
But is treacherous, sinful, and slimy, as Nye might hev well known before.

But she said that she knew
Where the Injins was hid,
And the statement was true,
For it seemed that she did,
Since she led William where he was covered by seventeen Modocs, and slid!

Then they reached for his hair;
But Nye sez, "By the law
Of nations, forbear!
I surrenders no more:
And I looks to be treated, you hear me? as a pris'ner, a pris'ner of war!"

But Captain Jack rose
And he sez, "It's too thin!
Such statements as those
It's too late to begin.
There's a MODOC INDICTMENT agin you, O Paleface, and you're goin' in!

"You stole Schonchin's squaw
In the year sixty-two;
It was in sixty-four
That Long Jack you went through,
And you burned Nasty Jim's rancheria, and his wives and his papooses too.

"This gun in my hand
Was sold me by you
'Gainst the law of the land,
And I grieves it is true!"
And he buried his face in his blanket and wept as he hid it from view.

"But you're tried and condemned,
And skelping's your doom,"
And he paused and he hemmed
But why this resume?
He was skelped 'gainst the custom of nations, and cut off like a rose in its bloom.

So I asks without guile,

And I trusts not in vain,
If this is the style
That is going to obtain
If here's Captain Jack still a-livin', and Nye with no skelp on his brain?

AN IDYL OF THE ROAD

(SIERRAS, 1876)

DRAMATIS PERSONAE

First Tourist
Second Tourist
Yuba Bill, Driver
A Stranger

FIRST TOURIST
Look how the upland plunges into cover,
Green where the pines fade sullenly away.
Wonderful those olive depths! and wonderful, moreover

SECOND TOURIST
The red dust that rises in a suffocating way.

FIRST TOURIST
Small is the soul that cannot soar above it,
Cannot but cling to its ever-kindred clay:
Better be yon bird, that seems to breathe and love it

SECOND TOURIST
Doubtless a hawk or some other bird of prey.
Were we, like him, as sure of a dinner
That on our stomachs would comfortably stay;
Or were the fried ham a shade or two just thinner,
That must confront us at closing of the day:
Then might you sing like Theocritus or Virgil,
Then might we each make a metrical essay;
But verse just now I must protest and urge ill
Fits a digestion by travel led astray.

CHORUS OF PASSENGERS
Speed, Yuba Bill! oh, speed us to our dinner!
Speed to the sunset that beckons far away.

SECOND TOURIST
William of Yuba, O Son of Nimshi, hearken!
Check thy profanity, but not thy chariot's play.
Tell us, O William, before the shadows darken,

Where, and, oh! how we shall dine? O William, say!

YUBA BILL
It ain't my fault, nor the Kumpeney's, I reckon,
Ye can't get ez square meal ez any on the Bay,
Up at you place, whar the senset 'pears to beckon
Ez thet sharp allows in his airy sort o' way.
Thar woz a place wor yer hash ye might hev wrestled,
Kept by a woman ez chipper ez a jay
Warm in her breast all the morning sunshine nestled;
Red on her cheeks all the evening's sunshine lay.

SECOND TOURIST
Praise is but breath, O chariot compeller!
Yet of that hash we would bid you farther say.

YUBA BILL
Thar woz a snipe, like you, a fancy tourist
Kem to that ranch ez if to make a stay,
Ran off the gal, and ruined jist the purist
Critter that lived

STRANGER (quietly)
You're a liar, driver!

YUBA BILL (reaching for his revolver).
Eh!
Here take my lines, somebody

CHORUS OF PASSENGERS
Hush, boys! listen!
Inside there's a lady! Remember! No affray!

YUBA BILL
Ef that man lives, the fault ain't mine or his'n.

STRANGER
Wait for the sunset that beckons far away,
Then as you will! But, meantime, friends, believe me,
Nowhere on earth lives a purer woman; nay,
If my perceptions do surely not deceive me,
She is the lady we have inside to-day.
As for the man, you see that blackened pine tree,
Up which the green vine creeps heavenward away!
He was that scarred trunk, and she the vine that sweetly
Clothed him with life again, and lifted

SECOND TOURIST
Yes; but pray
How know you this?

STRANGER
She's my wife.

YUBA BILL
The h-ll you say!

THOMPSON OF ANGELS
It is the story of Thompson, of Thompson, the hero of Angels.
Frequently drunk was Thompson, but always polite to the stranger;
Light and free was the touch of Thompson upon his revolver;
Great the mortality incident on that lightness and freedom.

Yet not happy or gay was Thompson, the hero of Angels;
Often spoke to himself in accents of anguish and sorrow,
"Why do I make the graves of the frivolous youth who in folly
Thoughtlessly pass my revolver, forgetting its lightness and freedom?

"Why in my daily walks does the surgeon drop his left eyelid,
The undertaker smile, and the sculptor of gravestone marbles
Lean on his chisel and gaze? I care not o'er much for attention;
Simple am I in my ways, save but for this lightness and freedom."

So spake that pensive man, this Thompson, the hero of Angels,
Bitterly smiled to himself, as he strode through the chapparal musing.
"Why, oh, why?" echoed the pines in the dark olive depth far resounding.
"Why, indeed?" whispered the sage brush that bent 'neath his feet non-elastic.

Pleasant indeed was that morn that dawned o'er the barroom at Angels,
Where in their manhood's prime was gathered the pride of the hamlet.
Six "took sugar in theirs," and nine to the barkeeper lightly
Smiled as they said, "Well, Jim, you can give us our regular fusil."

Suddenly as the gray hawk swoops down on the barnyard, alighting
Where, pensively picking their corn, the favorite pullets are gathered,
So in that festive bar-room dropped Thompson, the hero of Angels,
Grasping his weapon dread with his pristine lightness and freedom.

Never a word he spoke; divesting himself of his garments,
Danced the war-dance of the playful yet truculent Modoc,
Uttered a single whoop, and then, in the accents of challenge,
Spake: "Oh, behold in me a Crested Jay Hawk of the mountain."

Then rose a pallid man, a man sick with fever and ague;
Small was he, and his step was tremulous, weak, and uncertain;
Slowly a Derringer drew, and covered the person of Thompson;
Said in his feeblest pipe, "I'm a Bald-headed Snipe of the Valley."

As on its native plains the kangaroo, startled by hunters,
Leaps with successive bounds, and hurries away to the thickets,
So leaped the Crested Hawk, and quietly hopping behind him
Ran, and occasionally shot, that Bald-headed Snipe of the Valley.

Vain at the festive bar still lingered the people of Angels,
Hearing afar in the woods the petulant pop of the pistol;
Never again returned the Crested Jay Hawk of the mountains,
Never again was seen the Bald-headed Snipe of the Valley.

Yet in the hamlet of Angels, when truculent speeches are uttered,
When bloodshed and life alone will atone for some trifling misstatement,
Maidens and men in their prime recall the last hero of Angels,
Think of and vainly regret the Bald-headed Snipe of the Valley!

THE HAWK'S NEST

(SIERRAS)

We checked our pace, the red road sharply rounding;
We heard the troubled flow
Of the dark olive depths of pines resounding
A thousand feet below.

Above the tumult of the canyon lifted,
The gray hawk breathless hung,
Or on the hill a winged shadow drifted
Where furze and thorn-bush clung;

Or where half-way the mountain side was furrowed
With many a seam and scar;
Or some abandoned tunnel dimly burrowed,
A mole-hill seen so far.

We looked in silence down across the distant
Unfathomable reach:
A silence broken by the guide's consistent
And realistic speech.

"Walker of Murphy's blew a hole through Peters
For telling him he lied;
Then up and dusted out of South Hornitos
Across the Long Divide.

"We ran him out of Strong's, and up through Eden,
And 'cross the ford below,
And up this canyon (Peters' brother leadin'),
And me and Clark and Joe.

"He fou't us game: somehow I disremember
Jest how the thing kem round;
Some say 'twas wadding, some a scattered ember
From fires on the ground.

"But in one minute all the hill below him
Was just one sheet of flame;
Guardin' the crest, Sam Clark and I called to him,
And, well, the dog was game!

"He made no sign: the fires of hell were round him,
The pit of hell below.
We sat and waited, but we never found him;
And then we turned to go.

"And then you see that rock that's grown so bristly
With chapparal and tan
Suthin crep' out: it might hev been a grizzly
It might hev been a man;

"Suthin that howled, and gnashed its teeth, and shouted
In smoke and dust and flame;
Suthin that sprang into the depths about it,
Grizzly or man, but game!

"That's all! Well, yes, it does look rather risky,
And kinder makes one queer
And dizzy looking down. A drop of whiskey
Ain't a bad thing right here!"

HER LETTER

I'm sitting alone by the fire,
Dressed just as I came from the dance,
In a robe even YOU would admire,
It cost a cool thousand in France;
I'm be-diamonded out of all reason,
My hair is done up in a cue:
In short, sir, "the belle of the season"
Is wasting an hour upon you.

A dozen engagements I've broken;
I left in the midst of a set;
Likewise a proposal, half spoken,
That waits, on the stairs, for me yet.
They say he'll be rich, when he grows up,
And then he adores me indeed;
And you, sir, are turning your nose up,
Three thousand miles off as you read.

"And how do I like my position?"
"And what do I think of New York?"
"And now, in my higher ambition,

With whom do I waltz, flirt, or talk?"
"And isn't it nice to have riches,
And diamonds and silks, and all that?"
"And aren't they a change to the ditches
And tunnels of Poverty Flat?"

Well, yes, if you saw us out driving
Each day in the Park, four-in-hand,
If you saw poor dear mamma contriving
To look supernaturally grand,
If you saw papa's picture, as taken
By Brady, and tinted at that,
You'd never suspect he sold bacon
And flour at Poverty Flat.

And yet, just this moment, when sitting
In the glare of the grand chandelier,
In the bustle and glitter befitting
The "finest soiree of the year,"
In the mists of a gaze de Chambery,
And the hum of the smallest of talk,
Somehow, Joe, I thought of the "Ferry,"
And the dance that we had on "The Fork;"

Of Harrison's barn, with its muster
Of flags festooned over the wall;
Of the candles that shed their soft lustre
And tallow on head-dress and shawl;
Of the steps that we took to one fiddle,
Of the dress of my queer vis-a-vis;
And how I once went down the middle
With the man that shot Sandy McGee;

Of the moon that was quietly sleeping
On the hill, when the time came to go;
Of the few baby peaks that were peeping
From under their bedclothes of snow;
Of that ride that to me was the rarest;
Of the something you said at the gate.
Ah! Joe, then I wasn't an heiress
To "the best-paying lead in the State."

Well, well, it's all past; yet it's funny
To think, as I stood in the glare
Of fashion and beauty and money,
That I should be thinking, right there,
Of some one who breasted high water,
And swam the North Fork, and all that,
Just to dance with old Folinsbee's daughter,
The Lily of Poverty Flat.

But goodness! what nonsense I'm writing!
(Mamma says my taste still is low),
Instead of my triumphs reciting,
I'm spooning on Joseph, heigh-ho!
And I'm to be "finished" by travel,
Whatever's the meaning of that.
Oh, why did papa strike pay gravel
In drifting on Poverty Flat?

Good-night! here's the end of my paper;
Good-night! if the longitude please,
For maybe, while wasting my taper,
YOUR sun's climbing over the trees.
But know, if you haven't got riches,
And are poor, dearest Joe, and all that,
That my heart's somewhere there in the ditches,
And you've struck it, on Poverty Flat.

HIS ANSWER TO "HER LETTER"

(REPORTED BY TRUTHFUL JAMES)

Being asked by an intimate party,
Which the same I would term as a friend,
Though his health it were vain to call hearty,
Since the mind to deceit it might lend;
For his arm it was broken quite recent,
And there's something gone wrong with his lung,
Which is why it is proper and decent
I should write what he runs off his tongue.

First, he says, Miss, he's read through your letter
To the end, and "the end came too soon;"
That a "slight illness kept him your debtor,"
(Which for weeks he was wild as a loon);
That "his spirits are buoyant as yours is;"
That with you, Miss, he "challenges Fate,"
(Which the language that invalid uses
At times it were vain to relate).

And he says "that the mountains are fairer
For once being held in your thought;"
That each rock "holds a wealth that is rarer
Than ever by gold-seeker sought."
(Which are words he would put in these pages,
By a party not given to guile;
Though the claim not, at date, paying wages,
Might produce in the sinful a smile.)

He remembers the ball at the Ferry,
And the ride, and the gate, and the vow,
And the rose that you gave him, that very
Same rose he is "treasuring now."
(Which his blanket he's kicked on his trunk, Miss,
And insists on his legs being free
And his language to me from his bunk, Miss,
Is frequent and painful and free.)

He hopes you are wearing no willows,
But are happy and gay all the while;
That he knows (which this dodging of pillows
Imparts but small ease to the style,
And the same you will pardon) he knows, Miss,
That, though parted by many a mile,
Yet, were HE lying under the snows, Miss,
They'd melt into tears at your smile.

And "you'll still think of him in your pleasures,
In your brief twilight dreams of the past;
In this green laurel spray that he treasures,
It was plucked where your parting was last;
In this specimen, but a small trifle,
It will do for a pin for your shawl."
(Which, the truth not to wickedly stifle,
Was his last week's "clean up," and HIS ALL.)

He's asleep, which the same might seem strange, Miss,
Were it not that I scorn to deny
That I raised his last dose, for a change, Miss,
In view that his fever was high;
But he lies there quite peaceful and pensive.
And now, my respects, Miss, to you;
Which my language, although comprehensive,
Might seem to be freedom, is true.

For I have a small favor to ask you,
As concerns a bull-pup, and the same,
If the duty would not overtask you,
You would please to procure for me, GAME;
And send per express to the Flat, Miss,
For they say York is famed for the breed,
Which, though words of deceit may be that, Miss,
I'll trust to your taste, Miss, indeed.

P.S. Which this same interfering
Into other folks' way I despise;
Yet if it so be I was hearing
That it's just empty pockets as lies
Betwixt you and Joseph, it follers
That, having no family claims,

Here's my pile, which it's six hundred dollars,
As is YOURS, with respects,
TRUTHFUL JAMES.

"THE RETURN OF BELISARIUS"

(MUD FLAT, 1860)

So you're back from your travels, old fellow,
And you left but a twelvemonth ago;
You've hobnobbed with Louis Napoleon,
Eugenie, and kissed the Pope's toe.
By Jove, it is perfectly stunning,
Astounding, and all that, you know;
Yes, things are about as you left them
In Mud Flat a twelvemonth ago.

The boys! they're all right, Oh! Dick Ashley,
He's buried somewhere in the snow;
He was lost on the Summit last winter,
And Bob has a hard row to hoe.
You know that he's got the consumption?
You didn't! Well, come, that's a go;
I certainly wrote you at Baden,
Dear me! that was six months ago.

I got all your outlandish letters,
All stamped by some foreign P. O.
I handed myself to Miss Mary
That sketch of a famous chateau.
Tom Saunders is living at 'Frisco,
They say that he cuts quite a show.
You didn't meet Euchre-deck Billy
Anywhere on your road to Cairo?

So you thought of the rusty old cabin,
The pines, and the valley below,
And heard the North Fork of the Yuba
As you stood on the banks of the Po?
'Twas just like your romance, old fellow;
But now there is standing a row
Of stores on the site of the cabin
That you lived in a twelvemonth ago.

But it's jolly to see you, old fellow,
To think it's a twelvemonth ago!
And you have seen Louis Napoleon,
And look like a Johnny Crapaud.
Come in. You will surely see Mary,

You know we are married. What, no?
Oh, ay! I forgot there was something
Between you a twelvemonth ago.

FURTHER LANGUAGE FROM TRUTHFUL JAMES

(NYE'S FORD, STANISLAUS, 1870)

Do I sleep? do I dream?
Do I wonder and doubt?
Are things what they seem?
Or is visions about?
Is our civilization a failure?
Or is the Caucasian played out?

Which expressions are strong;
Yet would feebly imply
Some account of a wrong
Not to call it a lie
As was worked off on William, my pardner,
And the same being W. Nye.

He came down to the Ford
On the very same day
Of that lottery drawed
By those sharps at the Bay;
And he says to me, "Truthful, how goes it?"
I replied, "It is far, far from gay;

"For the camp has gone wild
On this lottery game,
And has even beguiled
'Injin Dick' by the same."
Then said Nye to me, "Injins is pizen:
But what is his number, eh, James?"

I replied, "7, 2,
9, 8, 4, is his hand;"
When he started, and drew
Out a list, which he scanned;
Then he softly went for his revolver
With language I cannot command.

Then I said, "William Nye!"
But he turned upon me,
And the look in his eye
Was quite painful to see;
And he says, "You mistake; this poor Injin
I protects from such sharps as YOU be!"

I was shocked and withdrew;
But I grieve to relate,
When he next met my view
Injin Dick was his mate;
And the two around town was a-lying
In a frightfully dissolute state.

Which the war dance they had
Round a tree at the Bend
Was a sight that was sad;
And it seemed that the end
Would not justify the proceedings,
As I quiet remarked to a friend.

For that Injin he fled
The next day to his band;
And we found William spread
Very loose on the strand,
With a peaceful-like smile on his features,
And a dollar greenback in his hand;

Which the same, when rolled out,
We observed, with surprise,
Was what he, no doubt,
Thought the number and prize
Them figures in red in the corner,
Which the number of notes specifies.

Was it guile, or a dream?
Is it Nye that I doubt?
Are things what they seem?
Or is visions about?
Is our civilization a failure?
Or is the Caucasian played out?

AFTER THE ACCIDENT

(MOUTH OF THE SHAFT)

What I want is my husband, sir,
And if you're a man, sir,
You'll give me an answer,
Where is my Joe?

Penrhyn, sir, Joe,
Caernarvonshire.
Six months ago
Since we came here

Eh? Ah, you know!

Well, I am quiet
And still,
But I must stand here,
And will!
Please, I'll be strong,
If you'll just let me wait
Inside o' that gate
Till the news comes along.

"Negligence!"
That was the cause!
Butchery!
Are there no laws,
Laws to protect such as we?

Well, then!
I won't raise my voice.
There, men!
I won't make no noise,
Only you just let me be.

Four, only four did he say
Saved! and the other ones? Eh?
Why do they call?
Why are they all
Looking and coming this way?

What's that? a message?
I'll take it.
I know his wife, sir,
I'll break it.
"Foreman!"
Ay, ay!
"Out by and by,
Just saved his life.
Say to his wife
Soon he'll be free."
Will I? God bless you!
It's me!

THE GHOST THAT JIM SAW

Why, as to that, said the engineer,
Ghosts ain't things we are apt to fear;
Spirits don't fool with levers much,
And throttle-valves don't take to such;
And as for Jim,

What happened to him
Was one half fact, and t'other half whim!

Running one night on the line, he saw
A house as plain as the moral law
Just by the moonlit bank, and thence
Came a drunken man with no more sense
Than to drop on the rail
Flat as a flail,
As Jim drove by with the midnight mail.

Down went the patents, steam reversed.
Too late! for there came a "thud." Jim cursed
As the fireman, there in the cab with him,
Kinder stared in the face of Jim,
And says, "What now?"
Says Jim, "What now!
I've just run over a man, that's how!"

The fireman stared at Jim. They ran
Back, but they never found house nor man,
Nary a shadow within a mile.
Jim turned pale, but he tried to smile,
Then on he tore
Ten mile or more,
In quicker time than he'd made afore.

Would you believe it! the very next night
Up rose that house in the moonlight white,
Out comes the chap and drops as before,
Down goes the brake and the rest encore;
And so, in fact,
Each night that act
Occurred, till folks swore Jim was cracked.

Humph! let me see; it's a year now, 'most,
That I met Jim, East, and says, "How's your ghost?"
"Gone," says Jim; "and more, it's plain
That ghost don't trouble me again.
I thought I shook
That ghost when I took
A place on an Eastern line, but look!

"What should I meet, the first trip out,
But the very house we talked about,
And the selfsame man! 'Well,' says I, 'I guess
It's time to stop this 'yer foolishness.'
So I crammed on steam,
When there came a scream
From my fireman, that jest broke my dream:

"'You've killed somebody!' Says I, 'Not much!
I've been thar often, and thar ain't no such,
And now I'll prove it!' Back we ran,
And darn my skin! but thar WAS a man
On the rail, dead,
Smashed in the head!
Now I call that meanness!" That's all Jim said.

"SEVENTY-NINE"

(MR. INTERVIEWER INTERVIEWED)

Know me next time when you see me, won't you, old smarty?
Oh, I mean YOU, old figger-head, just the same party!
Take out your pensivil, damn you; sharpen it, do!
Any complaints to make? Lots of 'em, one of 'em's YOU.

You! who are YOU, anyhow, goin' round in that sneakin' way?
Never in jail before, was you, old blatherskite, say?
Look at it; don't it look pooty? Oh, grin, and be damned to you, do!
But if I had you this side o' that gratin,' I'd just make it lively
for you.

How did I get in here? Well what 'ud you give to know?
'Twasn't by sneakin' round where I hadn't no call to go;
'Twasn't by hangin' round a-spyin' unfortnet men.
Grin! but I'll stop your jaw if ever you do that agen.

Why don't you say suthin, blast you? Speak your mind if you dare.
Ain't I a bad lot, sonny? Say it, and call it square.
Hain't got no tongue, hey, hev ye? Oh, guard! here's a little swell
A cussin' and swearin' and yellin', and bribin' me not to tell.

There! I thought that 'ud fetch ye! And you want to know my name?
"Seventy-nine" they call me, but that is their little game;
For I'm werry highly connected, as a gent, sir, can understand,
And my family hold their heads up with the very furst in the land.

For 'twas all, sir, a put-up job on a pore young man like me;
And the jury was bribed a puppos, and at furst they couldn't agree;
And I sed to the judge, sez I, Oh, grin! it's all right, my son!
But you're a werry lively young pup, and you ain't to be played upon!

Wot's that you got? tobacco? I'm cussed but I thought 'twas a tract.
Thank ye! A chap t'other day now, lookee, this is a fact
Slings me a tract on the evils o' keepin' bad company,
As if all the saints was howlin' to stay here along o' we.

No, I hain't no complaints. Stop, yes; do you see that chap,

Him standin' over there, a-hidin' his eyes in his cap?
Well, that man's stumick is weak, and he can't stand the pris'n fare;
For the coffee is just half beans, and the sugar it ain't nowhere.

Perhaps it's his bringin' up; but he's sickenin' day by day,
And he doesn't take no food, and I'm seein' him waste away.
And it isn't the thing to see; for, whatever he's been and done,
Starvation isn't the plan as he's to be saved upon.

For he cannot rough it like me; and he hasn't the stamps, I guess,
To buy him his extry grub outside o' the pris'n mess.
And perhaps if a gent like you, with whom I've been sorter free,
Would thank you! But, say! look here! Oh, blast it! don't give it
to ME!

Don't you give it to me; now, don't ye, don't ye, DON'T!
You think it's a put-up job; so I'll thank ye, sir, if you won't.
But hand him the stamps yourself: why, he isn't even my pal;
And, if it's a comfort to you, why, I don't intend that he shall.

THE STAGE-DRIVER'S STORY

It was the stage-driver's story, as he stood with his back to the wheelers,
Quietly flecking his whip, and turning his quid of tobacco;
While on the dusty road, and blent with the rays of the moonlight,
We saw the long curl of his lash and the juice of tobacco descending.

"Danger! Sir, I believe you, indeed, I may say, on that subject,
You your existence might put to the hazard and turn of a wager.
I have seen danger? Oh, no! not me, sir, indeed, I assure you:
'Twas only the man with the dog that is sitting alone in yon wagon.

"It was the Geiger Grade, a mile and a half from the summit:
Black as your hat was the night, and never a star in the heavens.
Thundering down the grade, the gravel and stones we sent flying
Over the precipice side, a thousand feet plumb to the bottom.

"Half-way down the grade I felt, sir, a thrilling and creaking,
Then a lurch to one side, as we hung on the bank of the canyon;
Then, looking up the road, I saw, in the distance behind me,
The off hind wheel of the coach, just loosed from its axle, and following.

"One glance alone I gave, then gathered together my ribbons,
Shouted, and flung them, outspread, on the straining necks of my cattle;
Screamed at the top of my voice, and lashed the air in my frenzy,
While down the Geiger Grade, on THREE wheels, the vehicle thundered.

"Speed was our only chance, when again came the ominous rattle:
Crack, and another wheel slipped away, and was lost in the darkness.

TWO only now were left; yet such was our fearful momentum,
Upright, erect, and sustained on TWO wheels, the vehicle thundered.

"As some huge boulder, unloosed from its rocky shelf on the mountain,
Drives before it the hare and the timorous squirrel, far leaping,
So down the Geiger Grade rushed the Pioneer coach, and before it
Leaped the wild horses, and shrieked in advance of the danger impending.

"But to be brief in my tale. Again, ere we came to the level,
Slipped from its axle a wheel; so that, to be plain in my statement,
A matter of twelve hundred yards or more, as the distance may be,
We traveled upon ONE wheel, until we drove up to the station.

"Then, sir, we sank in a heap; but, picking myself from the ruins,
I heard a noise up the grade; and looking, I saw in the distance
The three wheels following still, like moons on the horizon whirling,
Till, circling, they gracefully sank on the road at the side of the station.

"This is my story, sir; a trifle, indeed, I assure you.
Much more, perchance, might be said but I hold him of all men most lightly
Who swerves from the truth in his tale. No, thank you - Well, since you ARE pressing,
Perhaps I don't care if I do: you may give me the same, Jim, no sugar."

A QUESTION OF PRIVILEGE

REPORTED BY TRUTHFUL JAMES

It was Andrew Jackson Sutter who, despising Mr. Cutter for remarks
he heard him utter in debate upon the floor,
Swung him up into the skylight, in the peaceful, pensive twilight,
and then keerlessly proceeded, makin' no account what WE did
To wipe up with his person casual dust upon the floor.

Now a square fight never frets me, nor unpleasantness upsets me, but
the simple thing that gets me, now the job is done and gone,
And we've come home free and merry from the peaceful cemetery,
leavin' Cutter there with Sutter, that mebbe just a stutter
On the part of Mr. Cutter caused the loss we deeply mourn.

Some bashful hesitation, just like spellin' punctooation, might have
worked an aggravation on to Sutter's mournful mind,
For the witnesses all vary ez to wot was said and nary a galoot will
toot his horn except the way he is inclined.

But they all allow that Sutter had begun a kind of mutter, when
uprose Mr. Cutter with a sickening kind of ease,
And proceeded then to wade in to the subject then prevadin': "Is
Profanity degradin'?" in words like unto these:

"Onlike the previous speaker, Mr. Sutter of Yreka, he was but a
humble seeker and not like him, a cuss"
It was here that Mr. Sutter softly reached for Mr. Cutter, when the
latter with a stutter said: "ac-customed to discuss."

Then Sutter he rose grimly, and sorter smilin' dimly bowed onto the
Chairman primly (just like Cutter ez could be!)
Drawled "he guessed he must fall-back as Mr. Cutter owned the
Pack as he just had played the Jack as-" (here Cutter's gun
went crack! as Mr. Sutter gasped and ended) "every man can see!"

But William Henry Pryor, just in range of Sutter's fire, here
evinced a wild desire to do somebody harm,
And in the general scrimmage no one thought if Sutter's "image" was
a misplaced punctooation, like the hole in Pryor's arm.

For we all waltzed in together, never carin' to ask whether it was
Sutter or was Cutter we woz tryin' to abate.
But we couldn't help perceivin', when we took to inkstand heavin',
that the process was relievin' to the sharpness of debate,

So we've come home free and merry from the peaceful cemetery, and I
make no commentary on these simple childish games;
Things is various and human, and the man ain't born of woman who is
free to intermeddle with his pal's intents and aims.

THE THOUGHT-READER OF ANGELS

REPORTED BY TRUTHFUL JAMES

We hev tumbled ez dust
Or ez worms of the yearth;
Wot we looked for hez bust!
We are objects of mirth!
They have played us old Pards of the river! they hev played us for all we was worth!

Was it euchre or draw
Cut us off in our bloom?
Was it faro, whose law
Is uncertain ez doom?
Or an innocent "Jack pot" that opened was to us ez the jaws of the tomb?

It was nary! It kem
With some sharps from the States.
Ez folks sez, "All things kem
To the fellers ez waits;"
And we'd waited six months for that suthin' had me and Bill Nye—in such straits!

And it kem. It was small;

It was dream-like and weak;
It wore store clothes, that's all
That we knew, so to speak;
But it called itself "Billson, Thought-Reader" which ain't half a name for its cheek!

He could read wot you thought,
And he knew wot you did;
He could find things untaught,
No matter whar hid;
And he went to it, blindfold and smiling, being led by the hand like a kid!

Then I glanced at Bill Nye,
And I sez, without pride,
"You'll excuse US. We've nigh
On to nothin' to hide;
But if some gent will lend us a twenty, we'll hide it whar folks shall decide."

It was Billson's own self
Who forked over the gold,
With a smile. "Thar's the pelf,"
He remarked. "I make bold
To advance it, and go twenty better that I'll find it without being told."

Then I passed it to Nye,
Who repassed it to me.
And we bandaged each eye
Of that Billson ez we
Softly dropped that coin in his coat pocket, ez the hull crowd around us could see.

That was all. He'd one hand
Locked in mine. Then he groped.
We could not understand
Why that minit Nye sloped,
For we knew we'd the dead thing on Billson, even more than we dreamed of or hoped.

For he stood thar in doubt
With his hand to his head;
Then he turned, and lit out
Through the door where Nye fled,
Draggin' me and the rest of us arter, while we larfed till we thought we was dead,

Till he overtook Nye
And went through him. Words fail
For what follers! Kin I
Paint our agonized wail
Ez he drew from Nye's pocket that twenty wot we sworn was in his own coat-tail!

And it WAS! But, when found,
It proved bogus and brass!
And the question goes round
How the thing kem to pass?

Or, if PASSED, woz it passed thar by William; and I listens, and echoes "Alas!

"For the days when the skill
Of the keerds was no blind,
When no effort of will
Could beat four of a kind,
When the thing wot you held in your hand, Pard, was worth more than the thing in your mind."

THE SPELLING BEE AT ANGELS

(REPORTED BY TRUTHFUL JAMES)

Waltz in, waltz in, ye little kids, and gather round my knee,
And drop them books and first pot-hooks, and hear a yarn from me.
I kin not sling a fairy tale of Jinnys fierce and wild,
For I hold it is unchristian to deceive a simple child;
But as from school yer driftin' by, I thowt ye'd like to hear
Of a "Spelling Bee" at Angels that we organized last year.

It warn't made up of gentle kids, of pretty kids, like you,
But gents ez hed their reg'lar growth, and some enough for two.
There woz Lanky Jim of Sutter's Fork and Bilson of Lagrange,
And "Pistol Bob," who wore that day a knife by way of change.
You start, you little kids, you think these are not pretty names,
But each had a man behind it, and my name is Truthful James.

There was Poker Dick from Whisky Flat, and Smith of Shooter's Bend,
And Brown of Calaveras which I want no better friend;
Three-fingered Jack, yes, pretty dears, three fingers, YOU have five.
Clapp cut off two, it's sing'lar, too, that Clapp ain't now alive.
'Twas very wrong indeed, my dears, and Clapp was much to blame;
Likewise was Jack, in after-years, for shootin' of that same.

The nights was kinder lengthenin' out, the rains had jest begun,
When all the camp came up to Pete's to have their usual fun;
But we all sot kinder sad-like around the bar-room stove
Till Smith got up, permiskiss-like, and this remark he hove:
"Thar's a new game down in Frisco, that ez far ez I can see
Beats euchre, poker, and van-toon, they calls the 'Spellin' Bee.'"

Then Brown of Calaveras simply hitched his chair and spake,
"Poker is good enough for me," and Lanky Jim sez, "Shake!"
And Bob allowed he warn't proud, but he "must say right thar
That the man who tackled euchre hed his education squar."
This brought up Lenny Fairchild, the schoolmaster, who said
He knew the game, and he would give instructions on that head.

"For instance, take some simple word," sez he, "like 'separate:'
Now who can spell it?" Dog my skin, ef thar was one in eight.

This set the boys all wild at once. The chairs was put in row,
And at the head was Lanky Jim, and at the foot was Joe,
And high upon the bar itself the schoolmaster was raised,
And the bar-keep put his glasses down, and sat and silent gazed.

The first word out was "parallel," and seven let it be,
Till Joe waltzed in his "double l" betwixt the "a" and "e;"
For since he drilled them Mexicans in San Jacinto's fight
Thar warn't no prouder man got up than Pistol Joe that night
Till "rhythm" came! He tried to smile, then said "they had him there,"
And Lanky Jim, with one long stride, got up and took his chair.

O little kids, my pretty kids, 'twas touchin' to survey
These bearded men, with weppings on, like schoolboys at their play.
They'd laugh with glee, and shout to see each other lead the van,
And Bob sat up as monitor with a cue for a rattan,
Till the Chair gave out "incinerate," and Brown said he'd be durned
If any such blamed word as that in school was ever learned.

When "phthisis" came they all sprang up, and vowed the man who rung
Another blamed Greek word on them be taken out and hung.
As they sat down again I saw in Bilson's eye a flash,
And Brown of Calaveras was a-twistin' his mustache,
And when at last Brown slipped on "gneiss," and Bilson took his chair,
He dropped some casual words about some folks who dyed their hair.

And then the Chair grew very white, and the Chair said he'd adjourn,
But Poker Dick remarked that HE would wait and get his turn;
Then with a tremblin' voice and hand, and with a wanderin' eye,
The Chair next offered "eider-duck," and Dick began with "I",
And Bilson smiled, then Bilson shrieked! Just how the fight begun
I never knowed, for Bilson dropped, and Dick, he moved up one.

Then certain gents arose and said "they'd business down in camp,"
And "ez the road was rather dark, and ez the night was damp,
They'd" here got up Three-fingered Jack and locked the door and yelled:
"No, not one mother's son goes out till that thar word is spelled!"
But while the words were on his lips, he groaned and sank in pain,
And sank with Webster on his chest and Worcester on his brain.

Below the bar dodged Poker Dick, and tried to look ez he
Was huntin' up authorities thet no one else could see;
And Brown got down behind the stove, allowin' he "was cold,"
Till it upsot and down his legs the cinders freely rolled,
And several gents called "Order!" till in his simple way
Poor Smith began with "O-r" - "Or" - and he was dragged away.

O little kids, my pretty kids, down on your knees and pray!
You've got your eddication in a peaceful sort of way;
And bear in mind thar may be sharps ez slings their spellin' square,
But likewise slings their bowie-knives without a thought or care.

You wants to know the rest, my dears? Thet's all! In me you see
The only gent that lived to tell about the Spellin' Bee!

He ceased and passed, that truthful man; the children went their way
With downcast heads and downcast hearts but not to sport or play.
For when at eve the lamps were lit, and supperless to bed
Each child was sent, with tasks undone and lessons all unsaid,
No man might know the awful woe that thrilled their youthful frames,
As they dreamed of Angels Spelling Bee and thought of Truthful James.

ARTEMIS IN SIERRA

DRAMATIS PERSONAE

Poet. Philosopher. Jones of Mariposa.

POET
Halt! Here we are. Now wheel your mare a trifle
Just where you stand; then doff your hat and swear
Never yet was scene you might cover with your rifle
Half as complete or as marvelously fair.

PHILOSOPHER
Dropped from Olympus or lifted out of Tempe,
Swung like a censer betwixt the earth and sky!
He who in Greece sang of flocks and flax and hemp, he
Here might recall them, six thousand feet on high!

POET
Well you may say so. The clamor of the river,
Hum of base toil, and man's ignoble strife,
Halt far below, where the stifling sunbeams quiver,
But never climb to this purer, higher life!

Not to this glade, where Jones of Mariposa,
Simple and meek as his flocks we're looking at,
Tends his soft charge; nor where his daughter Rosa
(A shot.)
Hallo! What's that?

PHILOSOPHER
A something thro' my hat
Bullet, I think. You were speaking of his daughter?

POET
Yes; but your hat you were moving through the leaves;
Likely he thought it some eagle bent on slaughter.
Lightly he shoots (A second shot.)

PHILOSOPHER
As one readily perceives.
Still, he improves! This time YOUR hat has got it,
Quite near the band! Eh? Oh, just as you please
Stop, or go on.

POET
Perhaps we'd better trot it
Down through the hollow, and up among the trees.

BOTH
Trot, trot, trot, where the bullets cannot follow;
Trot down and up again among the laurel trees.

PHILOSOPHER
Thanks, that is better; now of this shot-dispensing
Jones and his girl, you were saying

POET
Well, you see
I, hang it all! Oh! what's the use of fencing!
Sir, I confess it! these shots were meant for ME.

PHILOSOPHER
Are you mad!

POET
God knows, I shouldn't wonder!
I love this coy nymph, who, coldly as yon peak
Shines on the river it feeds, yet keeps asunder
Long have I worshiped, but never dared to speak.

Till she, no doubt, her love no longer hiding,
Waked by some chance word her father's jealousy;
Slips her disdain as an avalanche down gliding
Sweeps flocks and kin away to clear a path for ME.

Hence his attack.

PHILOSOPHER
I see. What I admire
Chiefly, I think, in your idyl, so to speak,
Is the cool modesty that checks your youthful fire,
Absence of self-love and abstinence of cheek!

Still, I might mention, I've met the gentle Rosa,
Danced with her thrice, to her father's jealous dread;
And, it is possible, she's happened to disclose a
Ahem! You can fancy why he shoots at ME instead.

POET

YOU?

PHILOSOPHER
Me. But kindly take your hand from your revolver,
I am not choleric but accidents may chance.
And here's the father, who alone can be the solver
Of this twin riddle of the hat and the romance.

Enter JONES OF MARIPOSA.

POET
Speak, shepherd, mine!

PHILOSOPHER
Hail! Time-and-cartridge waster,
Aimless exploder of theories and skill!
Whom do you shoot?

JONES OF MARIPOSA
Well, shootin' ain't my taste, or
EF I shoot anything I only shoot to kill.

That ain't what's up. I only kem to tell ye
Sportin' or courtin' trot homeward for your life!
Gals will be gals, and p'r'aps it's just ez well ye
Larned there was one had no wish to be a wife.

POET
What?

PHILOSOPHER
Is this true?

JONES OF MARIPOSA
I reckon it looks like it.
She saw ye comin'. My gun was standin' by;
She made a grab, and 'fore I up could strike it,
Blazed at ye both! The critter is SO shy!

POET
Who?

JONES OF MARIPOSA
My darter!

PHILOSOPHER
Rosa?

JONES OF MARIPOSA
Same! Good-by!

JACK OF THE TULES

(SOUTHERN CALIFORNIA)

Shrewdly you question, Senor, and I fancy
You are no novice. Confess that to little
Of my poor gossip of Mission and Pueblo
You are a stranger!

Am I not right? Ah! believe me, that ever
Since we joined company at the posada
I've watched you closely, and pardon an old priest
I've caught you smiling!

Smiling to hear an old fellow like me talk
Gossip of pillage and robbers, and even
Air his opinion of law and alcaldes
Like any other!

Now! by that twist of the wrist on the bridle,
By that straight line from the heel to the shoulder,
By that curt speech, nay! nay! no offense, son,
You are a soldier?

No? Then a man of affairs? San Sebastian!
'Twould serve me right if I prattled thus wildly
To say a sheriff? No? just caballero?
Well, more's the pity.

Ah! what we want here's a man of your presence;
Sano, Secreto, yes, all the four S's,
Joined with a boldness and dash, when the time comes,
And may I say it?

One not TOO hard on the poor country people,
Peons and silly vaqueros, who, dazzled
By reckless skill, and, perchance, reckless largesse,
Wink at some queer things.

No? You would crush THEM as well as the robbers,
Root them out, scatter them? Ah you are bitter
And yet, quien sabe, perhaps that's the one way
To catch their leader.

As to myself, now, I'd share your displeasure;
For I admit in this Jack of the Tules
Certain good points. He still comes to confession
You'd "like to catch him"?

Ah, if you did at such times, you might lead him
Home by a thread. Good! Again you are smiling:
You have no faith in such shrift, and but little
In priest or penitent.

Bueno! We take no offense, sir; whatever
It please you to say, it becomes us, for Church sake,
To bear in peace. Yet, if you were kinder
And less suspicious

I might still prove to you, Jack of the Tules
Shames not our teaching; nay, even might show you,
Hard by this spot, his old comrade, who, wounded,
Lives on his bounty.

If, ah, you listen! I see I can trust you;
Then, on your word as a gentleman, follow.
Under that sycamore stands the old cabin;
There sits his comrade.

Eh! are you mad? You would try to ARREST him?
You, with a warrant? Oh, well, take the rest of them:
Pedro, Bill, Murray, Pat Doolan. Hey! all of you,
Tumble out, damn it!

There! that'll do, boys! Stand back! Ease his elbows;
Take the gag from his mouth. Good! Now scatter like devils
After his posse, four straggling, four drunken
At the posada.

You, help me off with these togs, and then vamos!
Now, ole Jeff Dobbs! Sheriff, Scout, and Detective!
You're so derned 'cute! Kinder sick, ain't ye, bluffing
Jack of the Tules!

IV. MISCELLANEOUS

A GREYPORT LEGEND

(1797)

They ran through the streets of the seaport town,
They peered from the decks of the ships that lay;
The cold sea-fog that came whitening down
Was never as cold or white as they.
"Ho, Starbuck and Pinckney and Tenterden!
Run for your shallops, gather your men,

Scatter your boats on the lower bay."

Good cause for fear! In the thick mid-day
The hulk that lay by the rotting pier,
Filled with the children in happy play,
Parted its moorings and drifted clear,
Drifted clear beyond reach or call,
Thirteen children they were in all,
All adrift in the lower bay!

Said a hard-faced skipper, "God help us all!
She will not float till the turning tide!"
Said his wife, "My darling will hear MY call,
Whether in sea or heaven she bide;"
And she lifted a quavering voice and high,
Wild and strange as a sea-bird's cry,
Till they shuddered and wondered at her side.

The fog drove down on each laboring crew,
Veiled each from each and the sky and shore:
There was not a sound but the breath they drew,
And the lap of water and creak of oar;
And they felt the breath of the downs, fresh blown
O'er leagues of clover and cold gray stone,
But not from the lips that had gone before.

They came no more. But they tell the tale
That, when fogs are thick on the harbor reef,
The mackerel fishers shorten sail
For the signal they know will bring relief;
For the voices of children, still at play
In a phantom hulk that drifts alway
Through channels whose waters never fail.

It is but a foolish shipman's tale,
A theme for a poet's idle page;
But still, when the mists of Doubt prevail,
And we lie becalmed by the shores of Age,
We hear from the misty troubled shore
The voice of the children gone before,
Drawing the soul to its anchorage.

A NEWPORT ROMANCE

They say that she died of a broken heart
(I tell the tale as 'twas told to me);
But her spirit lives, and her soul is part
Of this sad old house by the sea.

Her lover was fickle and fine and French:
It was nearly a hundred years ago
When he sailed away from her arms, poor wench!
With the Admiral Rochambeau.

I marvel much what periwigged phrase
Won the heart of this sentimental Quaker,
At what gold-laced speech of those modish days
She listened, the mischief take her!

But she kept the posies of mignonette
That he gave; and ever as their bloom failed
And faded (though with her tears still wet)
Her youth with their own exhaled.

Till one night, when the sea-fog wrapped a shroud
Round spar and spire and tarn and tree,
Her soul went up on that lifted cloud
From this sad old house by the sea.

And ever since then, when the clock strikes two,
She walks unbidden from room to room,
And the air is filled that she passes through
With a subtle, sad perfume.

The delicate odor of mignonette,
The ghost of a dead-and-gone bouquet,
Is all that tells of her story; yet
Could she think of a sweeter way?

I sit in the sad old house to-night,
Myself a ghost from a farther sea;
And I trust that this Quaker woman might,
In courtesy, visit me.

For the laugh is fled from porch and lawn,
And the bugle died from the fort on the hill,
And the twitter of girls on the stairs is gone,
And the grand piano is still.

Somewhere in the darkness a clock strikes two:
And there is no sound in the sad old house,
But the long veranda dripping with dew,
And in the wainscot a mouse.

The light of my study-lamp streams out
From the library door, but has gone astray
In the depths of the darkened hall. Small doubt
But the Quakeress knows the way.

Was it the trick of a sense o'erwrought

With outward watching and inward fret?
But I swear that the air just now was fraught
With the odor of mignonette!

I open the window, and seem almost
So still lies the ocean, to hear the beat
Of its Great Gulf artery off the coast,
And to bask in its tropic heat.

In my neighbor's windows the gas-lights flare,
As the dancers swing in a waltz of Strauss;
And I wonder now could I fit that air
To the song of this sad old house.

And no odor of mignonette there is,
But the breath of morn on the dewy lawn;
And mayhap from causes as slight as this
The quaint old legend is born.

But the soul of that subtle, sad perfume,
As the spiced embalmings, they say, outlast
The mummy laid in his rocky tomb,
Awakens my buried past.

And I think of the passion that shook my youth,
Of its aimless loves and its idle pains,
And am thankful now for the certain truth
That only the sweet remains.

And I hear no rustle of stiff brocade,
And I see no face at my library door;
For now that the ghosts of my heart are laid,
She is viewless for evermore.

But whether she came as a faint perfume,
Or whether a spirit in stole of white,
I feel, as I pass from the darkened room,
She has been with my soul to-night!

SAN FRANCISCO

(FROM THE SEA)

Serene, indifferent of Fate,
Thou sittest at the Western Gate;

Upon thy height, so lately won,
Still slant the banners of the sun;

Thou seest the white seas strike their tents,
O Warder of two continents!

And, scornful of the peace that flies
Thy angry winds and sullen skies,

Thou drawest all things, small, or great,
To thee, beside the Western Gate.

O lion's whelp, that hidest fast
In jungle growth of spire and mast!

I know thy cunning and thy greed,
Thy hard high lust and willful deed,

And all thy glory loves to tell
Of specious gifts material.

Drop down, O Fleecy Fog, and hide
Her skeptic sneer and all her pride!

Wrap her, O Fog, in gown and hood
Of her Franciscan Brotherhood.

Hide me her faults, her sin and blame;
With thy gray mantle cloak her shame!

So shall she, cowled, sit and pray
Till morning bears her sins away.

Then rise, O Fleecy Fog, and raise
The glory of her coming days;

Be as the cloud that flecks the seas
Above her smoky argosies;

When forms familiar shall give place
To stranger speech and newer face;

When all her throes and anxious fears
Lie hushed in the repose of years;

When Art shall raise and Culture lift
The sensual joys and meaner thrift,

And all fulfilled the vision we
Who watch and wait shall never see;

Who, in the morning of her race,
Toiled fair or meanly in our place,

But, yielding to the common lot,
Lie unrecorded and forgot.

THE MOUNTAIN HEART'S-EASE

By scattered rocks and turbid waters shifting,
By furrowed glade and dell,
To feverish men thy calm, sweet face uplifting,
Thou stayest them to tell

The delicate thought that cannot find expression,
For ruder speech too fair,
That, like thy petals, trembles in possession,
And scatters on the air.

The miner pauses in his rugged labor,
And, leaning on his spade,
Laughingly calls unto his comrade-neighbor
To see thy charms displayed.

But in his eyes a mist unwonted rises,
And for a moment clear
Some sweet home face his foolish thought surprises,
And passes in a tear,

Some boyish vision of his Eastern village,
Of uneventful toil,
Where golden harvests followed quiet tillage
Above a peaceful soil.

One moment only; for the pick, uplifting,
Through root and fibre cleaves,
And on the muddy current slowly drifting
Are swept by bruised leaves.

And yet, O poet, in thy homely fashion,
Thy work thou dost fulfill,
For on the turbid current of his passion
Thy face is shining still!

GRIZZLY

Coward, of heroic size,
In whose lazy muscles lies
Strength we fear and yet despise;
Savage, whose relentless tusks
Are content with acorn husks;

Robber, whose exploits ne'er soared
O'er the bee's or squirrel's hoard;
Whiskered chin and feeble nose,
Claws of steel on baby toes,
Here, in solitude and shade,
Shambling, shuffling plantigrade,
Be thy courses undismayed!

Here, where Nature makes thy bed,
Let thy rude, half-human tread
Point to hidden Indian springs,
Lost in ferns and fragrant grasses,
Hovered o'er by timid wings,
Where the wood-duck lightly passes,
Where the wild bee holds her sweets,
Epicurean retreats,
Fit for thee, and better than
Fearful spoils of dangerous man.
In thy fat-jowled deviltry
Friar Tuck shall live in thee;
Thou mayst levy tithe and dole;
Thou shalt spread the woodland cheer,
From the pilgrim taking toll;
Match thy cunning with his fear;
Eat, and drink, and have thy fill;
Yet remain an outlaw still!

MADRONO

Captain of the Western wood,
Thou that apest Robin Hood!
Green above thy scarlet hose,
How thy velvet mantle shows!
Never tree like thee arrayed,
O thou gallant of the glade!

When the fervid August sun
Scorches all it looks upon,
And the balsam of the pine
Drips from stem to needle fine,
Round thy compact shade arranged,
Not a leaf of thee is changed!

When the yellow autumn sun
Saddens all it looks upon,
Spreads its sackcloth on the hills,
Strews its ashes in the rills,
Thou thy scarlet hose dost doff,
And in limbs of purest buff

Challengest the sombre glade
For a sylvan masquerade.

Where, oh, where, shall he begin
Who would paint thee, Harlequin?
With thy waxen burnished leaf,
With thy branches' red relief,
With thy polytinted fruit,
In thy spring or autumn suit,
Where begin, and oh, where end,
Thou whose charms all art transcend?

COYOTE

Blown out of the prairie in twilight and dew,
Half bold and half timid, yet lazy all through;
Loath ever to leave, and yet fearful to stay,
He limps in the clearing, an outcast in gray.

A shade on the stubble, a ghost by the wall,
Now leaping, now limping, now risking a fall,
Lop-eared and large-jointed, but ever alway
A thoroughly vagabond outcast in gray.

Here, Carlo, old fellow, he's one of your kind,
Go, seek him, and bring him in out of the wind.
What! snarling, my Carlo! So even dogs may
Deny their own kin in the outcast in gray.

Well, take what you will, though it be on the sly,
Marauding or begging, I shall not ask why,
But will call it a dole, just to help on his way
A four-footed friar in orders of gray!

TO A SEA-BIRD

(SANTA CRUZ, 1869)

Sauntering hither on listless wings,
Careless vagabond of the sea,
Little thou heedest the surf that sings,
The bar that thunders, the shale that rings,
Give me to keep thy company.

Little thou hast, old friend, that's new;
Storms and wrecks are old things to thee;
Sick am I of these changes, too;

Little to care for, little to rue,
I on the shore, and thou on the sea.

All of thy wanderings, far and near,
Bring thee at last to shore and me;
All of my journeyings end them here:
This our tether must be our cheer,
I on the shore, and thou on the sea.

Lazily rocking on ocean's breast,
Something in common, old friend, have we:
Thou on the shingle seek'st thy nest,
I to the waters look for rest,
I on the shore, and thou on the sea.

WHAT THE CHIMNEY SANG

Over the chimney the night-wind sang
And chanted a melody no one knew;
And the Woman stopped, as her babe she tossed,
And thought of the one she had long since lost,
And said, as her teardrops back she forced,
"I hate the wind in the chimney."

Over the chimney the night-wind sang
And chanted a melody no one knew;
And the Children said, as they closer drew,
"'Tis some witch that is cleaving the black night through,
'Tis a fairy trumpet that just then blew,
And we fear the wind in the chimney."

Over the chimney the night-wind sang
And chanted a melody no one knew;
And the Man, as he sat on his hearth below,
Said to himself, "It will surely snow,
And fuel is dear and wages low,
And I'll stop the leak in the chimney."

Over the chimney the night-wind sang
And chanted a melody no one knew;
But the Poet listened and smiled, for he
Was Man and Woman and Child, all three,
And said, "It is God's own harmony,
This wind we hear in the chimney."

DICKENS IN CAMP

Above the pines the moon was slowly drifting,
The river sang below;
The dim Sierras, far beyond, uplifting
Their minarets of snow.

The roaring camp-fire, with rude humor, painted
The ruddy tints of health
On haggard face and form that drooped and fainted
In the fierce race for wealth;

Till one arose, and from his pack's scant treasure
A hoarded volume drew,
And cards were dropped from hands of listless leisure
To hear the tale anew.

And then, while round them shadows gathered faster,
And as the firelight fell,
He read aloud the book wherein the Master
Had writ of "Little Nell."

Perhaps 'twas boyish fancy, for the reader
Was youngest of them all,
But, as he read, from clustering pine and cedar
A silence seemed to fall;

The fir-trees, gathering closer in the shadows,
Listened in every spray,
While the whole camp with "Nell" on English meadows
Wandered and lost their way.

And so in mountain solitudes, o'ertaken
As by some spell divine
Their cares dropped from them like the needles shaken
From out the gusty pine.

Lost is that camp and wasted all its fire;
And he who wrought that spell?
Ah! towering pine and stately Kentish spire,
Ye have one tale to tell!

Lost is that camp, but let its fragrant story
Blend with the breath that thrills
With hop-vine's incense all the pensive glory
That fills the Kentish hills.

And on that grave where English oak and holly
And laurel wreaths entwine,
Deem it not all a too presumptuous folly,
This spray of Western pine!

July, 1870.

Beg your pardon, old fellow! I think
I was dreaming just now when you spoke.
The fact is, the musical clink
Of the ice on your wine-goblet's brink
A chord of my memory woke.

And I stood in the pasture-field where
Twenty summers ago I had stood;
And I heard in that sound, I declare,
The clinking of bells in the air,
Of the cows coming home from the wood.

Then the apple-bloom shook on the hill;
And the mullein-stalks tilted each lance;
And the sun behind Rapalye's mill
Was my uttermost West, and could thrill
Like some fanciful land of romance.

Then my friend was a hero, and then
My girl was an angel. In fine,
I drank buttermilk; for at ten
Faith asks less to aid her than when
At thirty we doubt over wine.

Ah, well, it DOES seem that I must
Have been dreaming just now when you spoke,
Or lost, very like, in the dust
Of the years that slow fashioned the crust
On that bottle whose seal you last broke.

Twenty years was its age, did you say?
Twenty years? Ah, my friend, it is true!
All the dreams that have flown since that day,
All the hopes in that time passed away,
Old friend, I've been drinking with you!

FATE

"The sky is clouded, the rocks are bare,
The spray of the tempest is white in air;
The winds are out with the waves at play,
And I shall not tempt the sea to-day.

"The trail is narrow, the wood is dim,

The panther clings to the arching limb;
And the lion's whelps are abroad at play,
And I shall not join in the chase to-day."

But the ship sailed safely over the sea,
And the hunters came from the chase in glee;
And the town that was builded upon a rock
Was swallowed up in the earthquake shock.

GRANDMOTHER TENTERDEN

(MASSACHUSETTS SHORE, 1800)

I mind it was but yesterday:
The sun was dim, the air was chill;
Below the town, below the hill,
The sails of my son's ship did fill,
My Jacob, who was cast away.

He said, "God keep you, mother dear,"
But did not turn to kiss his wife;
They had some foolish, idle strife;
Her tongue was like a two-edged knife,
And he was proud as any peer.

Howbeit that night I took no note
Of sea nor sky, for all was drear;
I marked not that the hills looked near,
Nor that the moon, though curved and clear,
Through curd-like scud did drive and float.

For with my darling went the joy
Of autumn woods and meadows brown;
I came to hate the little town;
It seemed as if the sun went down
With him, my only darling boy.

It was the middle of the night:
The wind, it shifted west-by-south,
It piled high up the harbor mouth;
The marshes, black with summer drouth,
Were all abroad with sea-foam white.

It was the middle of the night:
The sea upon the garden leapt,
And my son's wife in quiet slept,
And I, his mother, waked and wept,
When lo! there came a sudden light.

And there he stood! His seaman's dress
All wet and dripping seemed to be;
The pale blue fires of the sea
Dripped from his garments constantly,
I could not speak through cowardness.

"I come through night and storm," he said.
"Through storm and night and death," said he,
"To kiss my wife, if it so be
That strife still holds 'twixt her and me,
For all beyond is peace," he said.

"The sea is His, and He who sent
The wind and wave can soothe their strife
And brief and foolish is our life."
He stooped and kissed his sleeping wife,
Then sighed, and like a dream he went.

Now, when my darling kissed not me,
But her, his wife, who did not wake,
My heart within me seemed to break;
I swore a vow, nor thenceforth spake
Of what my clearer eyes did see.

And when the slow weeks brought him not,
Somehow we spake of aught beside:
For she, her hope upheld her pride;
And I, in me all hope had died,
And my son passed as if forgot.

It was about the next springtide:
She pined and faded where she stood,
Yet spake no word of ill or good;
She had the hard, cold Edwards' blood
In all her veins and so she died.

One time I thought, before she passed,
To give her peace; but ere I spake
Methought, "HE will be first to break
The news in heaven," and for his sake
I held mine back until the last.

And here I sit, nor care to roam;
I only wait to hear his call.
I doubt not that this day next fall
Shall see me safe in port, where all
And every ship at last comes home.

And you have sailed the Spanish Main,
And knew my Jacob?... Eh! Mercy!
Ah! God of wisdom! hath the sea

Yielded its dead to humble me?
My boy!... My Jacob!... Turn again!

GUILD'S SIGNAL

[William Guild was engineer of the train which on the 19th of April, 1813, plunged into Meadow Brook, on the line of the Stonington and Providence Railroad. It was his custom, as often as he passed his home, to whistle an "All's well" to his wife. He was found, after the disaster, dead, with his hand on the throttle-valve of his engine.]

Two low whistles, quaint and clear:
That was the signal the engineer
That was the signal that Guild, 'tis said
Gave to his wife at Providence,
As through the sleeping town, and thence,
Out in the night,
On to the light,
Down past the farms, lying white, he sped!

As a husband's greeting, scant, no doubt,
Yet to the woman looking out,
Watching and waiting, no serenade,
Love-song, or midnight roundelay
Said what that whistle seemed to say:
"To my trust true,
So, love, to you!
Working or waiting, good-night!" it said.

Brisk young bagmen, tourists fine,
Old commuters along the line,
Brakemen and porters glanced ahead,
Smiled as the signal, sharp, intense,
Pierced through the shadows of Providence:
"Nothing amiss
Nothing! it is
Only Guild calling his wife," they said.

Summer and winter the old refrain
Rang o'er the billows of ripening grain,
Pierced through the budding boughs o'erhead,
Flew down the track when the red leaves burned
Like living coals from the engine spurned;
Sang as it flew,
"To our trust true,
First of all, duty. Good-night!" it said.

And then, one night, it was heard no more
From Stonington over Rhode Island shore,
And the folk in Providence smiled and said

As they turned in their beds, "The engineer
Has once forgotten his midnight cheer."
ONE only knew,
To his trust true,
Guild lay under his engine, dead.

ASPIRING MISS DE LAINE

(A CHEMICAL NARRATIVE)

Certain facts which serve to explain
The physical charms of Miss Addie De Laine,
Who, as the common reports obtain,
Surpassed in complexion the lily and rose;
With a very sweet mouth and a retrousse nose;
A figure like Hebe's, or that which revolves
In a milliner's window, and partially solves
That question which mentor and moralist pains,
If grace may exist minus feeling or brains.

Of course the young lady had beaux by the score,
All that she wanted, what girl could ask more?
Lovers that sighed and lovers that swore,
Lovers that danced and lovers that played,
Men of profession, of leisure, and trade;
But one, who was destined to take the high part
Of holding that mythical treasure, her heart,
This lover, the wonder and envy of town,
Was a practicing chemist, a fellow called Brown.

I might here remark that 'twas doubted by many,
In regard to the heart, if Miss Addie had any;
But no one could look in that eloquent face,
With its exquisite outline and features of grace,
And mark, through the transparent skin, how the tide
Ebbed and flowed at the impulse of passion or pride,
None could look, who believed in the blood's circulation
As argued by Harvey, but saw confirmation
That here, at least, Nature had triumphed o'er art,
And as far as complexion went she had a heart.

But this par parenthesis. Brown was the man
Preferred of all others to carry her fan,
Hook her glove, drape her shawl, and do all that a belle
May demand of the lover she wants to treat well.
Folks wondered and stared that a fellow called Brown
Abstracted and solemn, in manner a clown,
Ill dressed, with a lingering smell of the shop
Should appear as her escort at party or hop.

Some swore he had cooked up some villainous charm,
Or love philter, not in the regular Pharm-
Acopoeia, and thus, from pure malice prepense,
Had bewitched and bamboozled the young lady's sense;
Others thought, with more reason, the secret to lie
In a magical wash or indelible dye;
While Society, with its censorious eye
And judgment impartial, stood ready to damn
What wasn't improper as being a sham.

For a fortnight the townfolk had all been agog
With a party, the finest the season had seen,
To be given in honor of Miss Pollywog,
Who was just coming out as a belle of sixteen.
The guests were invited; but one night before
A carriage drew up at the modest back door
Of Brown's lab'ratory, and, full in the glare
Of a big purple bottle, some closely veiled fair
Alighted and entered: to make matters plain,
Spite of veils and disguises, 'twas Addie De Laine.

As a bower for true love, 'twas hardly the one
That a lady would choose to be wooed in or won:
No odor of rose or sweet jessamine's sigh
Breathed a fragrance to hallow their pledge of troth by,
Nor the balm that exhales from the odorous thyme;
But the gaseous effusions of chloride of lime,
And salts, which your chemist delights to explain
As the base of the smell of the rose and the drain.
Think of this, O ye lovers of sweetness! and know
What you smell when you snuff up Lubin or Pinaud.

I pass by the greetings, the transports and bliss,
Which of course duly followed a meeting like this,
And come down to business, for such the intent
Of the lady who now o'er the crucible leant,
In the glow of a furnace of carbon and lime,
Like a fairy called up in the new pantomime,
And give but her words, as she coyly looked down
In reply to the questioning glances of Brown:
"I am taking the drops, and am using the paste,
And the little white powders that had a sweet taste,
Which you told me would brighten the glance of my eye,
And the depilatory, and also the dye,
And I'm charmed with the trial; and now, my dear Brown,
I have one other favor, now, ducky, don't frown,
Only one, for a chemist and genius like you
But a trifle, and one you can easily do.
Now listen: to-morrow, you know, is the night
Of the birthday soiree of that Pollywog fright;
And I'm to be there, and the dress I shall wear

Is TOO lovely; but" - "But what then, ma chere?"
Said Brown, as the lady came to a full stop,
And glanced round the shelves of the little back shop.
"Well, I want, I want something to fill out the skirt
To the proper dimensions, without being girt
In a stiff crinoline, or caged in a hoop
That shows through one's skirt like the bars of a coop;
Something light, that a lady may waltz in, or polk,
With a freedom that none but you masculine folk
Ever know. For, however poor woman aspires,
She's always bound down to the earth by these wires.
Are you listening? Nonsense! don't stare like a spoon,
Idiotic; some light thing, and spacious, and soon
Something like, well, in fact, something like a balloon!"

Here she paused; and here Brown, overcome by surprise,
Gave a doubting assent with still wondering eyes,
And the lady departed. But just at the door
Something happened, 'tis true, it had happened before
In this sanctum of science, a sibilant sound,
Like some element just from its trammels unbound,
Or two substances that their affinities found.

The night of the anxiously looked for soiree
Had come, with its fair ones in gorgeous array;
With the rattle of wheels and the tinkle of bells,
And the "How do ye do's" and the "Hope you are well's;"
And the crush in the passage, and last lingering look
You give as you hang your best hat on the hook;
The rush of hot air as the door opens wide;
And your entry, that blending of self-possessed pride
And humility shown in your perfect-bred stare
At the folk, as if wondering how they got there;
With other tricks worthy of Vanity Fair.
Meanwhile, the safe topic, the beat of the room,
Already was losing its freshness and bloom;
Young people were yawning, and wondering when
The dance would come off; and why didn't it then:
When a vague expectation was thrilling the crowd,
Lo! the door swung its hinges with utterance proud!
And Pompey announced, with a trumpet-like strain,
The entrance of Brown and Miss Addie De Laine.

She entered; but oh! how imperfect the verb
To express to the senses her movement superb!
To say that she "sailed in" more clearly might tell
Her grace in its buoyant and billowy swell.
Her robe was a vague circumambient space,
With shadowy boundaries made of point-lace;
The rest was but guesswork, and well might defy
The power of critical feminine eye

To define or describe: 'twere as futile to try
The gossamer web of the cirrus to trace,
Floating far in the blue of a warm summer sky.

'Midst the humming of praises and glances of beaux
That greet our fair maiden wherever she goes,
Brown slipped like a shadow, grim, silent, and black,
With a look of anxiety, close in her track.
Once he whispered aside in her delicate ear
A sentence of warning, it might be of fear:
"Don't stand in a draught, if you value your life."
(Nothing more, such advice might be given your wife
Or your sweetheart, in times of bronchitis and cough,
Without mystery, romance, or frivolous scoff.)
But hark to the music; the dance has begun.
The closely draped windows wide open are flung;
The notes of the piccolo, joyous and light,
Like bubbles burst forth on the warm summer night.
Round about go the dancers; in circles they fly;
Trip, trip, go their feet as their skirts eddy by;
And swifter and lighter, but somewhat too plain,
Whisks the fair circumvolving Miss Addie De Laine.
Taglioni and Cerito well might have pined
For the vigor and ease that her movements combined;
E'en Rigelboche never flung higher her robe
In the naughtiest city that's known on the globe.
'Twas amazing, 'twas scandalous; lost in surprise,
Some opened their mouths, and a few shut their eyes.

But hark! At the moment Miss Addie De Laine,
Circling round at the outer edge of an ellipse
Which brought her fair form to the window again,
From the arms of her partner incautiously slips!
And a shriek fills the air, and the music is still,
And the crowd gather round where her partner forlorn
Still frenziedly points from the wide window-sill
Into space and the night; for Miss Addie was gone!
Gone like the bubble that bursts in the sun;
Gone like the grain when the reaper is done;
Gone like the dew on the fresh morning grass;
Gone without parting farewell; and alas!
Gone with a flavor of hydrogen gas!

When the weather is pleasant, you frequently meet
A white-headed man slowly pacing the street;
His trembling hand shading his lack-lustre eye,
Half blind with continually scanning the sky.
Rumor points him as some astronomical sage,
Re-perusing by day the celestial page;
But the reader, sagacious, will recognize Brown,
Trying vainly to conjure his lost sweetheart down,

And learn the stern moral this story must teach,
That Genius may lift its love out of its reach.

A LEGEND OF COLOGNE

Above the bones
St. Ursula owns,
And those of the virgins she chaperons;
Above the boats,
And the bridge that floats,
And the Rhine and the steamers' smoky throats;
Above the chimneys and quaint-tiled roofs,
Above the clatter of wheels and hoofs;
Above Newmarket's open space,
Above that consecrated place
Where the genuine bones of the Magi seen are,
And the dozen shops of the real Farina;
Higher than even old Hohestrasse,
Whose houses threaten the timid passer,
Above them all,
Through scaffolds tall,
And spires like delicate limbs in splinters,
The great Cologne's
Cathedral stones
Climb through the storms of eight hundred winters.

Unfinished there,
In high mid-air
The towers halt like a broken prayer;
Through years belated,
Unconsummated,
The hope of its architect quite frustrated.
Its very youth
They say, forsooth,
With a quite improper purpose mated;
And every stone
With a curse of its own
Instead of that sermon Shakespeare stated,
Since the day its choir,
Which all admire,
By Cologne's Archbishop was consecrated.

Ah! THAT was a day,
One well might say,
To be marked with the largest, whitest stone
To be found in the towers of all Cologne!
Along the Rhine,
From old Rheinstein,
The people flowed like their own good wine.

From Rudesheim,
And Geisenheim,
And every spot that is known to rhyme;
From the famed Cat's Castle of St. Goarshausen,
To the pictured roofs of Assmannshausen,
And down the track,
From quaint Schwalbach
To the clustering tiles of Bacharach;
From Bingen, hence
To old Coblentz:
From every castellated crag,
Where the robber chieftains kept their "swag,"
The folk flowed in, and Ober-Cassel
Shone with the pomp of knight and vassal;
And pouring in from near and far,
As the Rhine to its bosom draws the Ahr,
Or takes the arm of the sober Mosel,
So in Cologne, knight, squire, and losel,
Choked up the city's gates with men
From old St. Stephen to Zint Marjen.

What had they come to see? Ah me!
I fear no glitter of pageantry,
Nor sacred zeal
For Church's weal,
Nor faith in the virgins' bones to heal;
Nor childlike trust in frank confession
Drew these, who, dyed in deep transgression,
Still in each nest
On every crest
Kept stolen goods in their possession;
But only their gout
For something new,
More rare than the "roast" of a wandering Jew;
Or to be exact
To see in fact
A Christian soul, in the very act
Of being damned, secundum artem,
By the devil, before a soul could part 'em.

For a rumor had flown
Throughout Cologne
That the church, in fact, was the devil's own;
That its architect
(Being long "suspect")
Had confessed to the Bishop that he had wrecked
Not only his OWN soul, but had lost
The VERY FIRST CHRISTIAN SOUL that crossed
The sacred threshold: and all, in fine,
For that very beautiful design
Of the wonderful choir

They were pleased to admire.
And really, he must be allowed to say
To speak in a purely business way
That, taking the ruling market prices
Of souls and churches, in such a crisis
It would be shown
And his Grace must own
It was really a BARGAIN for Cologne!

Such was the tale
That turned cheeks pale
With the thought that the enemy might prevail,
And the church doors snap
With a thunderclap
On a Christian soul in that devil's trap.
But a wiser few,
Who thought that they knew
Cologne's Archbishop, replied, "Pooh, pooh!
Just watch him and wait,
And as sure as fate,
You'll find that the Bishop will give checkmate."

One here might note
How the popular vote,
As shown in all legends and anecdote,
Declares that a breach
Of trust to o'erreach
The devil is something quite proper for each.
And, really, if you
Give the devil his due
In spite of the proverb it's something you'll rue.
But to lie and deceive him,
To use and to leave him,
From Job up to Faust is the way to receive him,
Though no one has heard
It ever averred
That the "Father of Lies" ever yet broke HIS word,
But has left this position,
In every tradition,
To be taken alone by the "truth-loving" Christian!
Bom! from the tower!
It is the hour!
The host pours in, in its pomp and power
Of banners and pyx,
And high crucifix,
And crosiers and other processional sticks,
And no end of Marys
In quaint reliquaries,
To gladden the souls of all true antiquaries;
And an Osculum Pacis
(A myth to the masses

Who trusted their bones more to mail and cuirasses)
All borne by the throng
Who are marching along
To the square of the Dom with processional song,
With the flaring of dips,
And bending of hips,
And the chanting of hundred perfunctory lips;
And some good little boys
Who had come up from Neuss
And the Quirinuskirche to show off their voice:
All march to the square
Of the great Dom, and there
File right and left, leaving alone and quite bare
A covered sedan,
Containing so ran
The rumor, the victim to take off the ban.

They have left it alone,
They have sprinkled each stone
Of the porch with a sanctified Eau de Cologne,
Guaranteed in this case
To disguise every trace
Of a sulphurous presence in that sacred place.
Two Carmelites stand
On the right and left hand
Of the covered sedan chair, to wait the command
Of the prelate to throw
Up the cover and show
The form of the victim in terror below.
There's a pause and a prayer,
Then the signal, and there
Is a WOMAN! by all that is good and is fair!

A woman! and known
To them all, one must own
TOO WELL KNOWN to the many, to-day to be shown
As a martyr, or e'en
As a Christian! A queen
Of pleasance and revel, of glitter and sheen;
So bad that the worst
Of Cologne spake up first,
And declared 'twas an outrage to suffer one curst,
And already a fief
Of the Satanic chief,
To martyr herself for the Church's relief.
But in vain fell their sneer
On the mob, who I fear
On the whole felt a strong disposition to cheer.

A woman! and there
She stands in the glare

Of the pitiless sun and their pitying stare,
A woman still young,
With garments that clung
To a figure, though wasted with passion and wrung
With remorse and despair,
Yet still passing fair,
With jewels and gold in her dark shining hair,
And cheeks that are faint
'Neath her dyes and her paint.
A woman most surely but hardly a saint!

She moves. She has gone
From their pity and scorn;
She has mounted alone
The first step of stone,
And the high swinging doors she wide open has thrown,
Then pauses and turns,
As the altar blaze burns
On her cheeks, and with one sudden gesture she spurns
Archbishop and Prior,
Knight, ladye, and friar,
And her voice rings out high from the vault of the choir.

"O men of Cologne!
What I WAS ye have known;
What I AM, as I stand here, One knoweth alone.
If it be but His will
I shall pass from Him still,
Lost, curst, and degraded, I reckon no ill;
If still by that sign
Of His anger divine
One soul shall be saved, He hath blessed more than mine.
O men of Cologne!
Stand forth, if ye own
A faith like to this, or more fit to atone,
And take ye my place,
And God give you grace
To stand and confront Him, like me, face to face!"

She paused. Yet aloof
They all stand. No reproof
Breaks the silence that fills the celestial roof.
One instant, no more
She halts at the door,
Then enters!... A flood from the roof to the floor
Fills the church rosy red.
She is gone!
But instead,
Who is this leaning forward with glorified head
And hands stretched to save?
Sure this is no slave

Of the Powers of Darkness, with aspect so brave!

They press to the door,
But too late! All is o'er.
Naught remains but a woman's form prone on the floor;
But they still see a trace
Of that glow in her face
That they saw in the light of the altar's high blaze
On the image that stands
With the babe in its hands
Enshrined in the churches of all Christian lands.

A Te Deum sung,
A censer high swung,
With praise, benediction, and incense wide-flung,
Proclaim that the CURSE
IS REMOVED and no worse
Is the Dom for the trial, in fact, the REVERSE;
For instead of their losing
A soul in abusing
The Evil One's faith, they gained one of his choosing.

Thus the legend is told:
You will find in the old
Vaulted aisles of the Dom, stiff in marble or cold
In iron and brass,
In gown and cuirass,
The knights, priests, and bishops who came to that Mass;
And high o'er the rest,
With her babe at her breast,
The image of Mary Madonna the blest.
But you look round in vain,
On each high pictured pane,
For the woman most worthy to walk in her train.

Yet, standing to-day
O'er the dust and the clay,
'Midst the ghosts of a life that has long passed away,
With the slow-sinking sun
Looking softly upon
That stained-glass procession, I scarce miss the one
That it does not reveal,
For I know and I feel
That these are but shadows, the woman was real!

THE TALE OF A PONY

Name of my heroine, simply "Rose;"
Surname, tolerable only in prose;

Habitat, Paris, that is where
She resided for change of air;
Aetat twenty; complexion fair;
Rich, good looking, and debonnaire;
Smarter than Jersey lightning. There!
That's her photograph, done with care.

In Paris, whatever they do besides,
EVERY LADY IN FULL DRESS RIDES!
Moire antiques you never meet
Sweeping the filth of a dirty street
But every woman's claim to ton
Depends upon
The team she drives, whether phaeton,
Landau, or britzka. Hence it's plain
That Rose, who was of her toilet vain,
Should have a team that ought to be
Equal to any in all Paris!

"Bring forth the horse!" The commissaire
Bowed, and brought Miss Rose a pair
Leading an equipage rich and rare.
Why doth that lovely lady stare?
Why? The tail of the off gray mare
Is bobbed, by all that's good and fair!
Like the shaving-brushes that soldiers wear,
Scarcely showing as much back hair
As Tam O'Shanter's "Meg," and there,
Lord knows, she'd little enough to spare.

That stare and frown the Frenchman knew,
But did as well-bred Frenchmen do:
Raised his shoulders above his crown,
Joined his thumbs with the fingers down,
And said, "Ah, Heaven!" then, "Mademoiselle,
Delay one minute, and all is well!"
He went, returned; by what good chance
These things are managed so well in France
I cannot say, but he made the sale,
And the bob-tailed mare had a flowing tail.

All that is false in this world below
Betrays itself in a love of show;
Indignant Nature hides her lash
In the purple-black of a dyed mustache;
The shallowest fop will trip in French,
The would-be critic will misquote Trench;
In short, you're always sure to detect
A sham in the things folks most affect;
Bean-pods are noisiest when dry,
And you always wink with your weakest eye:

And that's the reason the old gray mare
Forever had her tail in the air,
With flourishes beyond compare,
Though every whisk
Incurred the risk
Of leaving that sensitive region bare.
She did some things that you couldn't but feel
She wouldn't have done had her tail been real.

Champs Elysees: time, past five.
There go the carriages, look alive!
Everything that man can drive,
Or his inventive skill contrive,
Yankee buggy or English "chay,"
Dog-cart, droschky, and smart coupe,
A desobligeante quite bulky
(French idea of a Yankee sulky);
Band in the distance playing a march,
Footman standing stiff as starch;
Savans, lorettes, deputies, Arch-
Bishops, and there together range
Sous-lieutenants and cent-gardes (strange
Way these soldier-chaps make change),
Mixed with black-eyed Polish dames,
With unpronounceable awful names;
Laces tremble and ribbons flout,
Coachmen wrangle and gendarmes shout
Bless us! what is the row about?
Ah! here comes Rosy's new turnout!
Smart! You bet your life 'twas that!
Nifty! (short for magnificat).
Mulberry panels, heraldic spread,
Ebony wheels picked out with red,
And two gray mares that were thoroughbred:
No wonder that every dandy's head
Was turned by the turnout, and 'twas said
That Caskowhisky (friend of the Czar),
A very good whip (as Russians are),
Was tied to Rosy's triumphal car,
Entranced, the reader will understand,
By "ribbons" that graced her head and hand.

Alas! the hour you think would crown
Your highest wishes should let you down!
Or Fate should turn, by your own mischance,
Your victor's car to an ambulance,
From cloudless heavens her lightnings glance!
(And these things happen, even in France.)
And so Miss Rose, as she trotted by,
The cynosure of every eye,
Saw to her horror the off mare shy,

Flourish her tail so exceedingly high
That, disregarding the closest tie,
And without giving a reason why,
She flung that tail so free and frisky
Off in the face of Caskowhisky.

Excuses, blushes, smiles: in fine,
End of the pony's tail, and mine!

ON A CONE OF THE BIG TREES

(SEQUOIA GIGANTEA)

Brown foundling of the Western wood,
Babe of primeval wildernesses!
Long on my table thou hast stood
Encounters strange and rude caresses;
Perchance contented with thy lot,
Surroundings new, and curious faces,
As though ten centuries were not
Imprisoned in thy shining cases.

Thou bring'st me back the halcyon days
Of grateful rest, the week of leisure,
The journey lapped in autumn haze,
The sweet fatigue that seemed a pleasure,
The morning ride, the noonday halt,
The blazing slopes, the red dust rising,
And then the dim, brown, columned vault,
With its cool, damp, sepulchral spicing.

Once more I see the rocking masts
That scrape the sky, their only tenant
The jay-bird, that in frolic casts
From some high yard his broad blue pennant.
I see the Indian files that keep
Their places in the dusty heather,
Their red trunks standing ankle-deep
In moccasins of rusty leather.

I see all this, and marvel much
That thou, sweet woodland waif, art able
To keep the company of such
As throng thy friend's, the poet's, table:
The latest spawn the press hath cast,
The "modern popes," - "the later Byrons,"
Why, e'en the best may not outlast
Thy poor relation, Sempervirens.

Thy sire saw the light that shone
On Mohammed's uplifted crescent,
On many a royal gilded throne
And deed forgotten in the present;
He saw the age of sacred trees
And Druid groves and mystic larches;
And saw from forest domes like these
The builder bring his Gothic arches.

And must thou, foundling, still forego
Thy heritage and high ambition,
To lie full lowly and full low,
Adjusted to thy new condition?
Not hidden in the drifted snows,
But under ink-drops idly spattered,
And leaves ephemeral as those
That on thy woodland tomb were scattered?

Yet lie thou there, O friend! and speak
The moral of thy simple story:
Though life is all that thou dost seek,
And age alone thy crown of glory,
Not thine the only germs that fail
The purpose of their high creation,
If their poor tenements avail
For worldly show and ostentation.

LONE MOUNTAIN

(CEMETERY, SAN FRANCISCO)

This is that hill of awe
That Persian Sindbad saw,
The mount magnetic;
And on its seaward face,
Scattered along its base,
The wrecks prophetic.

Here come the argosies
Blown by each idle breeze,
To and fro shifting;
Yet to the hill of Fate
All drawing, soon or late,
Day by day drifting;

Drifting forever here
Barks that for many a year
Braved wind and weather;
Shallops but yesterday

Launched on yon shining bay,
Drawn all together.

This is the end of all:
Sun thyself by the wall,
O poorer Hindbad!
Envy not Sindbad's fame:
Here come alike the same
Hindbad and Sindbad.

ALNASCHAR

Here's yer toy balloons! All sizes!
Twenty cents for that. It rises
Jest as quick as that 'ere, Miss,
Twice as big. Ye see it is
Some more fancy. Make it square
Fifty for 'em both. That's fair.

That's the sixth I've sold since noon.
Trade's reviving. Just as soon
As this lot's worked off, I'll take
Wholesale figgers. Make or break,
That's my motto! Then I'll buy
In some first-class lottery
One half ticket, numbered right
As I dreamed about last night.

That'll fetch it. Don't tell me!
When a man's in luck, you see,
All things help him. Every chance
Hits him like an avalanche.
Here's your toy balloons, Miss. Eh?
You won't turn your face this way?
Mebbe you'll be glad some day.
With that clear ten thousand prize
This 'yer trade I'll drop, and rise
Into wholesale. No! I'll take
Stocks in Wall Street. Make or break,
That's my motto! With my luck,
Where's the chance of being stuck?
Call it sixty thousand, clear,
Made in Wall Street in one year.

Sixty thousand! Umph! Let's see!
Bond and mortgage'll do for me.
Good! That gal that passed me by
Scornful like, why, mebbe I
Some day'll hold in pawn, why not?

All her father's prop. She'll spot
What's my little game, and see
What I'm after's HER. He! he!

He! he! When she comes to sue
Let's see! What's the thing to do?
Kick her? No! There's the perliss!
Sorter throw her off like this.
Hello! Stop! Help! Murder! Hey!
There's my whole stock got away,
Kiting on the house-tops! Lost!
All a poor man's fortin! Cost?
Twenty dollars! Eh! What's this?
Fifty cents! God bless ye, Miss!

THE TWO SHIPS

As I stand by the cross on the lone mountain's crest,
Looking over the ultimate sea,
In the gloom of the mountain a ship lies at rest,
And one sails away from the lea:
One spreads its white wings on a far-reaching track,
With pennant and sheet flowing free;
One hides in the shadow with sails laid aback,
The ship that is waiting for me!

But lo! in the distance the clouds break away,
The Gate's glowing portals I see;
And I hear from the outgoing ship in the bay
The song of the sailors in glee.
So I think of the luminous footprints that bore
The comfort o'er dark Galilee,
And wait for the signal to go to the shore,
To the ship that is waiting for me.

ADDRESS

(OPENING OF THE CALIFORNIA THEATRE, SAN FRANCISCO, JANUARY 19, 1870)

Brief words, when actions wait, are well:
The prompter's hand is on his bell;
The coming heroes, lovers, kings,
Are idly lounging at the wings;
Behind the curtain's mystic fold
The glowing future lies unrolled;
And yet, one moment for the Past,
One retrospect, the first and last.

"The world's a stage," the Master said.
To-night a mightier truth is read:
Not in the shifting canvas screen,
The flash of gas or tinsel sheen;
Not in the skill whose signal calls
From empty boards baronial halls;
But, fronting sea and curving bay,
Behold the players and the play.

Ah, friends! beneath your real skies
The actor's short-lived triumph dies:
On that broad stage of empire won,
Whose footlights were the setting sun,
Whose flats a distant background rose
In trackless peaks of endless snows;
Here genius bows, and talent waits
To copy that but One creates.

Your shifting scenes: the league of sand,
An avenue by ocean spanned;
The narrow beach of straggling tents,
A mile of stately monuments;
Your standard, lo! a flag unfurled,
Whose clinging folds clasp half the world,
This is your drama, built on facts,
With "twenty years between the acts."

One moment more: if here we raise
The oft-sung hymn of local praise,
Before the curtain facts must sway;
HERE waits the moral of your play.
Glassed in the poet's thought, you view
What money can, yet cannot do;
The faith that soars, the deeds that shine,
Above the gold that builds the shrine.

And oh! when others take our place,
And Earth's green curtain hides our face,
Ere on the stage, so silent now,
The last new hero makes his bow:
So may our deeds, recalled once more
In Memory's sweet but brief encore,
Down all the circling ages run,
With the world's plaudit of "Well done!"

DOLLY VARDEN

Dear Dolly! who does not recall

The thrilling page that pictured all
Those charms that held our sense in thrall
Just as the artist caught her,
As down that English lane she tripped,
In bowered chintz, hat sideways tipped,
Trim-bodiced, bright-eyed, roguish-lipped,
The locksmith's pretty daughter?

Sweet fragment of the Master's art!
O simple faith! O rustic heart!
O maid that hath no counterpart
In life's dry, dog-eared pages!
Where shall we find thy like? Ah, stay!
Methinks I saw her yesterday
In chintz that flowered, as one might say,
Perennial for ages.

Her father's modest cot was stone,
Five stories high; in style and tone
Composite, and, I frankly own,
Within its walls revealing
Some certain novel, strange ideas:
A Gothic door with Roman piers,
And floors removed some thousand years,
From their Pompeian ceiling.

The small salon where she received
Was Louis Quatorze, and relieved
By Chinese cabinets, conceived
Grotesquely by the heathen;
The sofas were a classic sight,
The Roman bench (sedilia hight);
The chairs were French in gold and white,
And one Elizabethan.

And she, the goddess of that shrine,
Two ringed fingers placed in mine,
The stones were many carats fine,
And of the purest water,
Then dropped a curtsy, far enough
To fairly fill her cretonne puff
And show the petticoat's rich stuff
That her fond parent bought her.

Her speech was simple as her dress,
Not French the more, but English less,
She loved; yet sometimes, I confess,
I scarce could comprehend her.
Her manners were quite far from shy.
There was a quiet in her eye
Appalling to the Hugh who'd try

With rudeness to offend her.

"But whence," I cried, "this masquerade?
Some figure for to-night's charade,
A Watteau shepherdess or maid?"
She smiled and begged my pardon:
"Why, surely you must know the name,
That woman who was Shakespeare's flame
Or Byron's, well, it's all the same:
Why, Lord! I'm Dolly Varden!"

TELEMACHUS VERSUS MENTOR

Don't mind me, I beg you, old fellow, I'll do very well here alone;
You must not be kept from your "German" because I've dropped in like a stone.
Leave all ceremony behind you, leave all thought of aught but yourself;
And leave, if you like, the Madeira, and a dozen cigars on the shelf.

As for me, you will say to your hostess, well, I scarcely need give you a cue.
Chant my praise! All will list to Apollo, though Mercury pipe to a few.
Say just what you please, my dear boy; there's more eloquence lies in youth's rash
Outspoken heart-impulse than ever growled under this grizzling mustache.

Go, don the dress coat of our tyrant, youth's panoplied armor for fight,
And tie the white neckcloth that rumples, like pleasure, and lasts but a night;
And pray the Nine Gods to avert you what time the Three Sisters shall frown,
And you'll lose your high-comedy figure, and sit more at ease in your gown.

He's off! There's his foot on the staircase. By Jove, what a bound! Really now
Did I ever leap like this springald, with Love's chaplet green on my brow?
Was I such an ass? No, I fancy. Indeed, I remember quite plain
A gravity mixed with my transports, a cheerfulness softened my pain.

He's gone! There's the slam of his cab door, there's the clatter of hoofs and the wheels;
And while he the light toe is tripping, in this armchair I'll tilt up my heels.
He's gone, and for what? For a tremor from a waist like a teetotum spun;
For a rosebud that's crumpled by many before it is gathered by one.

Is there naught in the halo of youth but the glow of a passionate race,
'Midst the cheers and applause of a crowd, to the goal of a beautiful face?
A race that is not to the swift, a prize that no merits enforce,
But is won by some faineant youth, who shall simply walk over the course?

Poor boy! shall I shock his conceit? When he talks of her cheek's loveliness,
Shall I say 'twas the air of the room, and was due to carbonic excess?
That when waltzing she drooped on his breast, and the veins of her eyelids grew dim,
'Twas oxygen's absence she felt, but never the presence of him?

Shall I tell him first love is a fraud, a weakling that's strangled in birth,

Recalled with perfunctory tears, but lost in unsanctified mirth?
Or shall I go bid him believe in all womankind's charm, and forget
In the light ringing laugh of the world the rattlesnake's gay castanet?

Shall I tear out a leaf from my heart, from that book that forever is shut
On the past? Shall I speak of my first love, Augusta, my Lalage?
But I forget. Was it really Augusta? No. 'Twas Lucy! No. Mary! No. Di!
Never mind! they were all first and faithless, and yet, I've forgotten just why.

No, no! Let him dream on and ever. Alas! he will waken too soon;
And it doesn't look well for October to always be preaching at June.
Poor boy! All his fond foolish trophies pinned yonder, a bow from HER hair,
A few billets-doux, invitations, and what's this? My name, I declare!

Humph! "You'll come, for I've got you a prize, with beauty and money no end:
You know her, I think; 'twas on dit she once was engaged to your friend;
But she says that's all over." Ah, is it? Sweet Ethel! Incomparable maid!
Or what if the thing were a trick? this letter so freely displayed!

My opportune presence! No! nonsense! Will nobody answer the bell?
Call a cab! Half past ten. Not too late yet. Oh, Ethel! Why don't you go? Well?
"Master said you would wait" Hang your master! "Have I ever a message to send?"
Yes, tell him I've gone to the German to dance with the friend of his friend.

WHAT THE WOLF REALLY SAID TO LITTLE RED RIDING-HOOD

Wondering maiden, so puzzled and fair,
Why dost thou murmur and ponder and stare?
"Why are my eyelids so open and wild?"
Only the better to see with, my child!
Only the better and clearer to view
Cheeks that are rosy and eyes that are blue.

Dost thou still wonder, and ask why these arms
Fill thy soft bosom with tender alarms,
Swaying so wickedly? Are they misplaced
Clasping or shielding some delicate waist?
Hands whose coarse sinews may fill you with fear
Only the better protect you, my dear!

Little Red Riding-Hood, when in the street,
Why do I press your small hand when we meet?
Why, when you timidly offered your cheek,
Why did I sigh, and why didn't I speak?
Why, well: you see, if the truth must appear
I'm not your grandmother, Riding-Hood, dear!

"So she's here, your unknown Dulcinea, the lady you met on the train,
And you really believe she would know you if you were to meet her again?"

"Of course," he replied, "she would know me; there never was womankind yet
Forgot the effect she inspired. She excuses, but does not forget."

"Then you told her your love?" asked the elder. The younger looked up with a smile:
"I sat by her side half an hour, what else was I doing the while?

"What, sit by the side of a woman as fair as the sun in the sky,
And look somewhere else lest the dazzle flash back from your own to her eye?

"No, I hold that the speech of the tongue be as frank and as bold as the look,
And I held up herself to herself, that was more than she got from her book."

"Young blood!" laughed the elder; "no doubt you are voicing the mode of To-Day:
But then we old fogies at least gave the lady some chance for delay.

"There's my wife (you must know), we first met on the journey from Florence to Rome:
It took me three weeks to discover who was she and where was her home;

"Three more to be duly presented; three more ere I saw her again;
And a year ere my romance BEGAN where yours ended that day on the train."

"Oh, that was the style of the stage-coach; we travel to-day by express;
Forty miles to the hour," he answered, "won't admit of a passion that's less."

"But what if you make a mistake?" quoth the elder. The younger half sighed.
"What happens when signals are wrong or switches misplaced?" he replied.

"Very well, I must bow to your wisdom," the elder returned, "but submit
Your chances of winning this woman your boldness has bettered no whit.

"Why, you do not at best know her name. And what if I try your ideal
With something, if not quite so fair, at least more en regle and real?

"Let me find you a partner. Nay, come, I insist, you shall follow, this way.
My dear, will you not add your grace to entreat Mr. Rapid to stay?

"My wife, Mr. Rapid Eh, what! Why, he's gone, yet he said he would come.
How rude! I don't wonder, my dear, you are properly crimson and dumb!"

O joy of creation
To be!
O rapture to fly

And be free!
Be the battle lost or won,
Though its smoke shall hide the sun,
I shall find my love, the one
Born for me!

I shall know him where he stands,
All alone,
With the power in his hands
Not o'erthrown;
I shall know him by his face,
By his godlike front and grace;
I shall hold him for a space,
All my own!

It is he, O my love!
So bold!
It is I, all thy love
Foretold!
It is I. O love! what bliss!
Dost thou answer to my kiss?
O sweetheart! what is this
Lieth there so cold?

THE OLD CAMP-FIRE

Now shift the blanket pad before your saddle back you fling,
And draw your cinch up tighter till the sweat drops from the ring:
We've a dozen miles to cover ere we reach the next divide.
Our limbs are stiffer now than when we first set out to ride,
And worse, the horses know it, and feel the leg-grip tire,
Since in the days when, long ago, we sought the old camp-fire.

Yes, twenty years! Lord! how we'd scent its incense down the trail,
Through balm of bay and spice of spruce, when eye and ear would fail,
And worn and faint from useless quest we crept, like this, to rest,
Or, flushed with luck and youthful hope, we rode, like this, abreast.
Ay! straighten up, old friend, and let the mustang think he's nigher,
Through looser rein and stirrup strain, the welcome old camp-fire.

You know the shout that would ring out before us down the glade,
And start the blue jays like a flight of arrows through the shade,
And sift the thin pine needles down like slanting, shining rain,
And send the squirrels scampering back to their holes again,
Until we saw, blue-veiled and dim, or leaping like desire,
That flame of twenty years ago, which lit the old camp-fire.

And then that rest on Nature's breast, when talk had dropped, and slow
The night wind went from tree to tree with challenge soft and low!

We lay on lazy elbows propped, or stood to stir the flame,
Till up the soaring redwood's shaft our shadows danced and came,
As if to draw us with the sparks, high o'er its unseen spire,
To the five stars that kept their ward above the old camp-fire,

Those picket stars whose tranquil watch half soothed, half shamed our sleep.
What recked we then what beasts or men around might lurk or creep?
We lay and heard with listless ears the far-off panther's cry,
The near coyote's snarling snap, the grizzly's deep-drawn sigh,
The brown bear's blundering human tread, the gray wolves' yelping choir
Beyond the magic circle drawn around the old camp-fire.

And then that morn! Was ever morn so filled with all things new?
The light that fell through long brown aisles from out the kindling blue,
The creak and yawn of stretching boughs, the jay-bird's early call,
The rat-tat-tat of woodpecker that waked the woodland hall,
The fainter stir of lower life in fern and brake and brier,
Till flashing leaped the torch of Day from last night's old camp-fire!

Well, well! we'll see it once again; we should be near it now;
It's scarce a mile to where the trail strikes off to skirt the slough,
And then the dip to Indian Spring, the wooded rise, and strange!
Yet here should stand the blasted pine that marked our farther range;
And here, what's this? A ragged swab of ruts and stumps and mire!
Sure this is not the sacred grove that hid the old camp-fire!

Yet here's the "blaze" I cut myself, and there's the stumbling ledge,
With quartz "outcrop" that lay atop, now leveled to its edge,
And mounds of moss-grown stumps beside the woodman's rotting chips,
And gashes in the hillside, that gape with dumb red lips.
And yet above the shattered wreck and ruin, curling higher
Ah yes! still lifts the smoke that marked the welcome old camp-fire!

Perhaps some friend of twenty years still lingers there to raise
To weary hearts and tired eyes that beacon of old days.
Perhaps but stay; 'tis gone! and yet once more it lifts as though
To meet our tardy blundering steps, and seems to MOVE, and lo!
Whirls by us in a rush of sound, the vanished funeral pyre
Of hopes and fears that twenty years burned in the old camp-fire!

For see, beyond the prospect spreads, with chimney, spire, and roof,
Two iron bands across the trail clank to our mustang's hoof;
Above them leap two blackened threads from limb-lopped tree to tree,
To where the whitewashed station speeds its message to the sea.
Rein in! Rein in! The quest is o'er. The goal of our desire
Is but the train whose track has lain across the old camp-fire!

THE STATION-MASTER OF LONE PRAIRIE

An empty bench, a sky of grayest etching,
A bare, bleak shed in blackest silhouette,
Twelve years of platform, and before them stretching
Twelve miles of prairie glimmering through the wet.

North, south, east, west, the same dull gray persistence,
The tattered vapors of a vanished train,
The narrowing rails that meet to pierce the distance,
Or break the columns of the far-off rain.

Naught but myself; nor form nor figure breaking
The long hushed level and stark shining waste;
Nothing that moves to fill the vision aching,
When the last shadow fled in sullen haste.

Nothing beyond. Ah yes! From out the station
A stiff, gaunt figure thrown against the sky,
Beckoning me with some wooden salutation
Caught from his signals as the train flashed by;

Yielding me place beside him with dumb gesture
Born of that reticence of sky and air.
We sit apart, yet wrapped in that one vesture
Of silence, sadness, and unspoken care:

Each following his own thought, around us darkening
The rain-washed boundaries and stretching track,
Each following those dim parallels and hearkening
For long-lost voices that will not come back.

Until, unasked, I knew not why or wherefore,
He yielded, bit by bit, his dreary past,
Like gathered clouds that seemed to thicken there for
Some dull down-dropping of their care at last.

Long had he lived there. As a boy had started
From the stacked corn the Indian's painted face;
Heard the wolves' howl the wearying waste that parted
His father's hut from the last camping-place.

Nature had mocked him: thrice had claimed the reaping,
With scythe of fire, of lands she once had sown;
Sent the tornado, round his hearthstone heaping
Rafters, dead faces that were like his own.

Then came the War Time. When its shadow beckoned
He had walked dumbly where the flag had led
Through swamp and fen, unknown, unpraised, unreckoned,
To famine, fever, and a prison bed.

Till the storm passed, and the slow tide returning

Cast him, a wreck, beneath his native sky;
Here, at his watch, gave him the chance of earning
Scant means to live, who won the right to die.

All this I heard, or seemed to hear, half blending
With the low murmur of the coming breeze,
The call of some lost bird, and the unending
And tireless sobbing of those grassy seas.

Until at last the spell of desolation
Broke with a trembling star and far-off cry.
The coming train! I glanced around the station,
All was as empty as the upper sky!

Naught but myself; nor form nor figure waking
The long hushed level and stark shining waste;
Naught but myself, that cry, and the dull shaking
Of wheel and axle, stopped in breathless haste!

"Now, then, look sharp! Eh, what? The Station-Master?
THAR'S NONE! We stopped here of our own accord.
The man got killed in that down-train disaster
This time last evening. Right there! All aboard!"

THE MISSION BELLS OF MONTEREY

O bells that rang, O bells that sang
Above the martyrs' wilderness,
Till from that reddened coast-line sprang
The Gospel seed to cheer and bless,
What are your garnered sheaves to-day?
O Mission bells! Eleison bells!
O Mission bells of Monterey!

O bells that crash, O bells that clash
Above the chimney-crowded plain,
On wall and tower your voices dash,
But never with the old refrain;
In mart and temple gone astray!
Ye dangle bells! Ye jangle bells!
Ye wrangle bells of Monterey!

O bells that die, so far, so nigh,
Come back once more across the sea;
Not with the zealot's furious cry,
Not with the creed's austerity;
Come with His love alone to stay,
O Mission bells! Eleison bells!
O Mission bells of Monterey!

"CROTALUS"

(RATTLESNAKE BAR, SIERRAS)

No life in earth, or air, or sky;
The sunbeams, broken silently,
On the bared rocks around me lie,

Cold rocks with half-warmed lichens scarred,
And scales of moss; and scarce a yard
Away, one long strip, yellow-barred.

Lost in a cleft! 'Tis but a stride
To reach it, thrust its roots aside,
And lift it on thy stick astride!

Yet stay! That moment is thy grace!
For round thee, thrilling air and space,
A chattering terror fills the place!

A sound as of dry bones that stir
In the dead Valley! By yon fir
The locust stops its noonday whir!

The wild bird hears; smote with the sound,
As if by bullet brought to ground,
On broken wing, dips, wheeling round!

The hare, transfixed, with trembling lip,
Halts, breathless, on pulsating hip,
And palsied tread, and heels that slip.

Enough, old friend! 'tis thou. Forget
My heedless foot, nor longer fret
The peace with thy grim castanet!

I know thee! Yes! Thou mayst forego
That lifted crest; the measured blow
Beyond which thy pride scorns to go,

Or yet retract! For me no spell
Lights those slit orbs, where, some think, dwell
Machicolated fires of hell!

I only know thee humble, bold,
Haughty, with miseries untold,
And the old Curse that left thee cold,

And drove thee ever to the sun,
On blistering rocks; nor made thee shun
Our cabin's hearth, when day was done,

And the spent ashes warmed thee best;
We knew thee, silent, joyless guest
Of our rude ingle. E'en thy quest

Of the rare milk-bowl seemed to be
Naught but a brother's poverty,
And Spartan taste that kept thee free

From lust and rapine. Thou! whose fame
Searchest the grass with tongue of flame,
Making all creatures seem thy game;

When the whole woods before thee run,
Asked but when all was said and done
To lie, untrodden, in the sun!

ON WILLIAM FRANCIS BARTLETT

DEAD AT PITTSFIELD, MASS., 1876

O poor Romancer, thou whose printed page,
Filled with rude speech and ruder forms of strife,
Was given to heroes in whose vulgar rage
No trace appears of gentler ways and life!

Thou who wast wont of commoner clay to build
Some rough Achilles or some Ajax tall;
Thou whose free brush too oft was wont to gild
Some single virtue till it dazzled all;

What right hast thou beside this laureled bier
Whereon all manhood lies, whereon the wreath
Of Harvard rests, the civic crown, and here
The starry flag, and sword and jeweled sheath?

Seest thou these hatchments? Knowest thou this blood
Nourished the heroes of Colonial days
Sent to the dim and savage-haunted wood
Those sad-eyed Puritans with hymns of praise?

Look round thee! Everywhere is classic ground.
There Greylock rears. Beside yon silver "Bowl"
Great Hawthorne dwelt, and in its mirror found
Those quaint, strange shapes that filled his poet's soul.

Still silent, Stranger? Thou who now and then
Touched the too credulous ear with pathos, canst not speak?
Hast lost thy ready skill of tongue and pen?
What, Jester! Tears upon that painted cheek?

Pardon, good friends! I am not here to mar
His laureled wreaths with this poor tinseled crown
This man who taught me how 'twas better far
To be the poem than to write it down.

I bring no lesson. Well have others preached
This sword that dealt full many a gallant blow;
I come once more to touch the hand that reached
Its knightly gauntlet to the vanquished foe.

O pale Aristocrat, that liest there,
So cold, so silent! Couldst thou not in grace
Have borne with us still longer, and so spare
The scorn we see in that proud, placid face?

"Hail and farewell!" So the proud Roman cried
O'er his dead hero. "Hail," but not "farewell."
With each high thought thou walkest side by side;
We feel thee, touch thee, know who wrought the spell!

THE BIRDS OF CIRENCESTER

Did I ever tell you, my dears, the way
That the birds of Cisseter "Cisseter!" eh?
Well "Ciren-cester" one OUGHT to say,
From "Castra," or "Caster,"
As your Latin master
Will further explain to you some day;
Though even the wisest err,
And Shakespeare writes "Ci-cester,"
While every visitor
Who doesn't say "Cissiter"
Is in "Ciren-cester" considered astray.

A hundred miles from London town
Where the river goes curving and broadening down
From tree-top to spire, and spire to mast,
Till it tumbles outright in the Channel at last
A hundred miles from that flat foreshore
That the Danes and the Northmen haunt no more
There's a little cup in the Cotswold hills
Which a spring in a meadow bubbles and fills,
Spanned by a heron's wing, crossed by a stride
Calm and untroubled by dreams of pride,

Guiltless of Fame or ambition's aims,
That is the source of the lordly Thames!
Remark here again that custom contemns
Both "Tames" and Thames, you must SAY "Tems!"
But WHY? no matter! from them you can see
Cirencester's tall spires loom up o'er the lea.

A. D. Five Hundred and Fifty-two,
The Saxon invaders, a terrible crew
Had forced the lines of the Britons through;
And Cirencester, half mud and thatch,
Dry and crisp as a tinder match,
Was fiercely beleaguered by foes, who'd catch
At any device that could harry and rout
The folk that so boldly were holding out.

For the streets of the town, as you'll see to-day
Were twisted and curved in a curious way
That kept the invaders still at bay;
And the longest bolt that a Saxon drew
Was stopped ere a dozen of yards it flew,
By a turn in the street, and a law so true
That even these robbers of all laws scorners!
Knew you couldn't shoot arrows AROUND street corners.

So they sat them down on a little knoll,
And each man scratched his Saxon poll,
And stared at the sky, where, clear and high,
The birds of that summer went singing by,
As if, in his glee, each motley jester
Were mocking the foes of Cirencester,
Till the jeering crow and the saucy linnet
Seemed all to be saying: "Ah! you're not in it!"

High o'er their heads the mavis flew,
And the "ouzel-cock so black of hue;"
And the "throstle," with his "note so true"
(You remember what Shakespeare says HE knew);
And the soaring lark, that kept dropping through
Like a bucket spilling in wells of blue;
And the merlin, seen on heraldic panes
With legs as vague as the Queen of Spain's;

And the dashing swift that would ricochet
From the tufts of grasses before them, yet
Like bold Antaeus, would each time bring
New life from the earth, barely touched by his wing;
And the swallow and martlet that always knew
The straightest way home. Here a Saxon churl drew
His breath, tapped his forehead, an idea had got through!

So they brought them some nets, which straightway they filled
With the swallows and martlets, the sweet birds who build
In the houses of man, all that innocent guild
Who sing at their labor on eaves and in thatch
And they stuck on their feathers a rude lighted match
Made of resin and tow. Then they let them all go
To be free! As a child-like diversion? Ah, no!
To work Cirencester's red ruin and woe.

For straight to each nest they flew, in wild quest
Of their homes and their fledgelings, that they loved the best;
And straighter than arrow of Saxon e'er sped
They shot o'er the curving streets, high overhead,
Bringing fire and terror to roof tree and bed,
Till the town broke in flame, wherever they came,
To the Briton's red ruin, the Saxon's red shame!

Yet they're all gone together! To-day you'll dig up
From "mound" or from "barrow" some arrow or cup.
Their fame is forgotten, their story is ended
'Neath the feet of the race they have mixed with and blended.
But the birds are unchanged, the ouzel-cock sings,
Still gold on his crest and still black on his wings;
And the lark chants on high, as he mounts to the sky,
Still brown in his coat and still dim in his eye;
While the swallow or martlet is still a free nester
In the eaves and the roofs of thrice-built Cirencester.

LINES TO A PORTRAIT, BY A SUPERIOR PERSON

When I bought you for a song,
Years ago, Lord knows how long!
I was struck, I may be wrong
By your features,
And a something in your air
That I couldn't quite compare
To my other plain or fair
Fellow creatures.

In your simple, oval frame
You were not well known to fame,
But to me 'twas all the same
Whoe'er drew you;
For your face I can't forget,
Though I oftentimes regret
That, somehow, I never yet
Saw quite through you.

Yet each morning, when I rise,

I go first to greet your eyes;
And, in turn, YOU scrutinize
My presentment.
And when shades of evening fall,
As you hang upon my wall,
You're the last thing I recall
With contentment.

It is weakness, yet I know
That I never turned to go
Anywhere, for weal or woe,
But I lingered
For one parting, thrilling flash
From your eyes, to give that dash
To the curl of my mustache,
That I fingered.

If to some you may seem plain,
And when people glance again
Where you hang, their lips refrain.
From confession;
Yet they turn in stealth aside,
And I note, they try to hide
How much they are satisfied
In expression.

Other faces I have seen;
Other forms have come between;
Other things I have, I ween,
Done and dared for!
But OUR ties they cannot sever,
And, though I should say it never,
You're the only one I ever
Really cared for!

And you'll still be hanging there
When we're both the worse for wear,
And the silver's on my hair
And off your backing;
Yet my faith shall never pass
In my dear old shaving-glass,
Till my face and yours, alas!
Both are lacking!

HER LAST LETTER

BEING A REPLY TO "HIS ANSWER"

June 4th! Do you know what that date means?

June 4th! By this air and these pines!
Well, only you know how I hate scenes,
These might be my very last lines!
For perhaps, sir, you'll kindly remember
If some OTHER things you've forgot
That you last wrote the 4th of DECEMBER,
Just six months ago I, from this spot;

From this spot, that you said was "the fairest
For once being held in my thought."
Now, really I call that the barest
Of, well, I won't say what I ought!
For here I am back from my "riches,"
My "triumphs," my "tours," and all that;
And YOU'RE not to be found in the ditches
Or temples of Poverty Flat!

From Paris we went for the season
To London, when pa wired, "Stop."
Mama says "his HEALTH" was the reason.
(I've heard that some things took a "drop.")
But she said if my patience I'd summon
I could go back with him to the Flat
Perhaps I was thinking of some one
Who of me, well, was not thinking THAT!

Of course you will SAY that I "never
Replied to the letter you wrote."
That is just like a man! But, however,
I read it or how could I quote?
And as to the stories you've heard (No,
Don't tell me you haven't, I know!),
You'll not believe one blessed word, Joe;
But just whence they came, let them go!

And they came from Sade Lotski of Yolo,
Whose father sold clothes on the Bar
You called him Job-lotski, you know, Joe,
And the boys said HER value was par.
Well, we met her in Paris just flaring
With diamonds, and lost in a hat
And she asked me "how Joseph was faring
In his love-suit on Poverty Flat!"

She thought it would shame me! I met her
With a look, Joe, that made her eyes drop;
And I said that your "love-suit fared better
Than any suit out of THEIR shop!"
And I didn't blush THEN as I'm doing
To find myself here, all alone,
And left, Joe, to do all the "sueing"

To a lover that's certainly flown.

In this brand-new hotel, called "The Lily"
(I wonder who gave it that name?)
I really am feeling quite silly,
To think I was once called the same;
And I stare from its windows, and fancy
I'm labeled to each passer-by.
Ah! gone is the old necromancy,
For nothing seems right to my eye.

On that hill there are stores that I knew not;
There's a street where I once lost my way;
And the copse where you once tied my shoe-knot
Is shamelessly open as day!
And that bank by the spring I once drank there,
And you called the place Eden, you know;
Now I'm banished like Eve though the bank there
Is belonging to "Adams and Co."

There's the rustle of silk on the sidewalk;
Just now there passed by a tall hat;
But there's gloom in this "boom" and this wild talk
Of the "future" of Poverty Flat.
There's a decorous chill in the air, Joe,
Where once we were simple and free;
And I hear they've been making a mayor, Joe,
Of the man who shot Sandy McGee.

But there's still the "lap, lap" of the river;
There's the song of the pines, deep and low.
(How my longing for them made me quiver
In the park that they call Fontainebleau!)
There's the snow-peak that looked on our dances,
And blushed when the morning said, "Go!"
There's a lot that remains which one fancies
But somehow there's never a Joe!

Perhaps, on the whole, it is better,
For you might have been changed like the rest;
Though it's strange that I'm trusting this letter
To papa, just to have it addressed.
He thinks he may find you, and really
Seems kinder now I'm all alone.
You might have been here, Joe, if merely
To LOOK what I'm willing to OWN.

Well, well! that's all past; so good-night, Joe;
Good-night to the river and Flat;
Good-night to what's wrong and what's right, Joe;
Good-night to the past, and all that

To Harrison's barn, and its dancers;
To the moon, and the white peak of snow;
And good-night to the canyon that answers
My "Joe!" with its echo of "No!"

P. S.

I've just got your note. You deceiver!
How dared you, how COULD you? Oh, Joe!
To think I've been kept a believer
In things that were six months ago!
And it's YOU'VE built this house, and the bank, too,
And the mills, and the stores, and all that!
And for everything changed I must thank YOU,
Who have "struck it" on Poverty Flat!

How dared you get rich, you great stupid!
Like papa, and some men that I know,
Instead of just trusting to Cupid
And to me for your money? Ah, Joe!
Just to think you sent never a word, dear,
Till you wrote to papa for consent!
Now I know why they had me transferred here,
And "the health of papa" what THAT meant!

Now I know why they call this "The Lily;"
Why the man who shot Sandy McGee
You made mayor! 'Twas because, oh, you silly!
He once "went down the middle" with me!
I've been fooled to the top of my bent here,
So come, and ask pardon, you know
That you've still got to get MY consent, dear!
And just think what that echo said Joe!

V. PARODIES

BEFORE THE CURTAIN

Behind the footlights hangs the rusty baize,
A trifle shabby in the upturned blaze
Of flaring gas and curious eyes that gaze.

The stage, methinks, perhaps is none too wide,
And hardly fit for royal Richard's stride,
Or Falstaff's bulk, or Denmark's youthful pride.

Ah, well! no passion walks its humble boards;

O'er it no king nor valiant Hector lords:
The simplest skill is all its space affords.

The song and jest, the dance and trifling play,
The local hit at follies of the day,
The trick to pass an idle hour away,

For these no trumpets that announce the Moor,
No blast that makes the hero's welcome sure,
A single fiddle in the overture!

TO THE PLIOCENE SKULL

(A GEOLOGICAL ADDRESS)

"Speak, O man, less recent! Fragmentary fossil!
Primal pioneer of pliocene formation,
Hid in lowest drifts below the earliest stratum
Of volcanic tufa!

"Older than the beasts, the oldest Palaeotherium;
Older than the trees, the oldest Cryptogami;
Older than the hills, those infantile eruptions
Of earth's epidermis!

"Eo – Mio – Plio - whatsoe'er the 'cene' was
That those vacant sockets filled with awe and wonder,
Whether shores Devonian or Silurian beaches,
Tell us thy strange story!

"Or has the professor slightly antedated
By some thousand years thy advent on this planet,
Giving thee an air that's somewhat better fitted
For cold-blooded creatures?

"Wert thou true spectator of that mighty forest
When above thy head the stately Sigillaria
Reared its columned trunks in that remote and distant
Carboniferous epoch?

"Tell us of that scene, the dim and watery woodland,
Songless, silent, hushed, with never bird or insect,
Veiled with spreading fronds and screened with tall club mosses,
Lycopodiacea,

"When beside thee walked the solemn Plesiosaurus,
And around thee crept the festive Ichthyosaurus,
While from time to time above thee flew and circled
Cheerful Pterodactyls.

"Tell us of thy food, those half-marine refections,
Crinoids on the shell and Brachipods au naturel,
Cuttlefish to which the pieuvre of Victor Hugo
Seems a periwinkle.

"Speak, thou awful vestige of the earth's creation,
Solitary fragment of remains organic!
Tell the wondrous secret of thy past existence,
Speak! thou oldest primate!"

Even as I gazed, a thrill of the maxilla,
And a lateral movement of the condyloid process,
With post-pliocene sounds of healthy mastication,
Ground the teeth together.

And from that imperfect dental exhibition,
Stained with express juices of the weed nicotian,
Came these hollow accents, blent with softer murmurs
Of expectoration:

"Which my name is Bowers, and my crust was busted
Falling down a shaft in Calaveras County;
But I'd take it kindly if you'd send the pieces
Home to old Missouri!"

* See notes 2

THE BALLAD OF MR. COOKE

(LEGEND OF THE CLIFF HOUSE, SAN FRANCISCO)

Where the sturdy ocean breeze
Drives the spray of roaring seas,
That the Cliff House balconies
Overlook:
There, in spite of rain that balked,
With his sandals duly chalked,
Once upon a tight-rope walked
Mr. Cooke.

But the jester's lightsome mien,
And his spangles and his sheen,
All had vanished when the scene
He forsook.
Yet in some delusive hope,
In some vague desire to cope,
ONE still came to view the rope
Walked by Cooke.

Amid Beauty's bright array,
On that strange eventful day,
Partly hidden from the spray,
In a nook,
Stood Florinda Vere de Vere;
Who, with wind-disheveled hair,
And a rapt, distracted air,
Gazed on Cooke.

Then she turned, and quickly cried
To her lover at her side,
While her form with love and pride
Wildly shook:
"Clifford Snook! oh, hear me now!
Here I break each plighted vow;
There's but one to whom I bow,
And that's Cooke!"

Haughtily that young man spoke:
"I descend from noble folk;
'Seven Oaks,' and then 'Se'nnoak,'
Lastly 'Snook,'
Is the way my name I trace.
Shall a youth of noble race
In affairs of love give place
To a Cooke?"

"Clifford Snook, I know thy claim
To that lineage and name,
And I think I've read the same
In Horne Tooke;
But I swear, by all divine,
Never, never, to be thine,
Till thou canst upon yon line
Walk like Cooke."

Though to that gymnastic feat
He no closer might compete
Than to strike a BALANCE-sheet
In a book;
Yet thenceforward from that day
He his figure would display
In some wild athletic way,
After Cooke.

On some household eminence,
On a clothes-line or a fence,
Over ditches, drains, and thence
O'er a brook,
He, by high ambition led,

Ever walked and balanced,
Till the people, wondering, said,
"How like Cooke!"

Step by step did he proceed,
Nerved by valor, not by greed,
And at last the crowning deed
Undertook.
Misty was the midnight air,
And the cliff was bleak and bare,
When he came to do and dare,
Just like Cooke.

Through the darkness, o'er the flow,
Stretched the line where he should go,
Straight across as flies the crow
Or the rook.
One wild glance around he cast;
Then he faced the ocean blast,
And he strode the cable last
Touched by Cooke.

Vainly roared the angry seas,
Vainly blew the ocean breeze;
But, alas! the walker's knees
Had a crook;
And before he reached the rock
Did they both together knock,
And he stumbled with a shock
Unlike Cooke!

Downward dropping in the dark,
Like an arrow to its mark,
Or a fish-pole when a shark
Bites the hook,
Dropped the pole he could not save,
Dropped the walker, and the wave
Swift engulfed the rival brave
Of J. Cooke!

Came a roar across the sea
Of sea-lions in their glee,
In a tongue remarkably
Like Chinook;
And the maddened sea-gull seemed
Still to utter, as he screamed,
"Perish thus the wretch who deemed
Himself Cooke!"

But on misty moonlit nights
Comes a skeleton in tights,

Walks once more the giddy heights
He mistook;
And unseen to mortal eyes,
Purged of grosser earthly ties,
Now at last in spirit guise
Outdoes Cooke.

Still the sturdy ocean breeze
Sweeps the spray of roaring seas,
Where the Cliff House balconies
Overlook;
And the maidens in their prime,
Reading of this mournful rhyme,
Weep where, in the olden time,
Walked J. Cooke.

THE BALLAD OF THE EMEU

Oh, say, have you seen at the Willows so green
So charming and rurally true
A singular bird, with a manner absurd,
Which they call the Australian Emeu?
Have you
Ever seen this Australian Emeu?

It trots all around with its head on the ground,
Or erects it quite out of your view;
And the ladies all cry, when its figure they spy,
"Oh! what a sweet pretty Emeu!
Oh! do
Just look at that lovely Emeu!"

One day to this spot, when the weather was hot,
Came Matilda Hortense Fortescue;
And beside her there came a youth of high name,
Augustus Florell Montague:
The two
Both loved that wild, foreign Emeu.

With two loaves of bread then they fed it, instead
Of the flesh of the white Cockatoo,
Which once was its food in that wild neighborhood
Where ranges the sweet Kangaroo,
That too
Is game for the famous Emeu!

Old saws and gimlets but its appetite whets,
Like the world-famous bark of Peru;
There's nothing so hard that the bird will discard,

And nothing its taste will eschew
That you
Can give that long-legged Emeu!

The time slipped away in this innocent play,
When up jumped the bold Montague:
"Where's that specimen pin that I gayly did win
In raffle, and gave unto you,
Fortescue?"
No word spoke the guilty Emeu!

"Quick! tell me his name whom thou gavest that same,
Ere these hands in thy blood I imbrue!"
"Nay, dearest," she cried, as she clung to his side,
"I'm innocent as that Emeu!"
"Adieu!"
He replied, "Miss M. H. Fortescue!"

Down she dropped at his feet, all as white as a sheet,
As wildly he fled from her view;
He thought 'twas her sin, for he knew not the pin
Had been gobbled up by the Emeu;
All through
The voracity of that Emeu!

MRS. JUDGE JENKINS

(BEING THE ONLY GENUINE SEQUEL TO "MAUD MULLER")

Maud Muller all that summer day
Raked the meadow sweet with hay;

Yet, looking down the distant lane,
She hoped the Judge would come again.

But when he came, with smile and bow,
Maud only blushed, and stammered, "Ha-ow?"

And spoke of her "pa," and wondered whether
He'd give consent they should wed together.

Old Muller burst in tears, and then
Begged that the Judge would lend him "ten;"

For trade was dull, and wages low,
And the "craps," this year, were somewhat slow.

And ere the languid summer died,
Sweet Maud became the Judge's bride.

But on the day that they were mated,
Maud's brother Bob was intoxicated;

And Maud's relations, twelve in all,
Were very drunk at the Judge's hall.

And when the summer came again,
The young bride bore him babies twain;

And the Judge was blest, but thought it strange
That bearing children made such a change;

For Maud grew broad and red and stout,
And the waist that his arm once clasped about

Was more than he now could span; and he
Sighed as he pondered, ruefully,

How that which in Maud was native grace
In Mrs. Jenkins was out of place;

And thought of the twins, and wished that they
Looked less like the men who raked the hay

On Muller's farm, and dreamed with pain
Of the day he wandered down the lane.

And looking down that dreary track,
He half regretted that he came back;

For, had he waited, he might have wed
Some maiden fair and thoroughbred;

For there be women fair as she,
Whose verbs and nouns do more agree.

Alas for maiden! alas for judge!
And the sentimental, that's one-half "fudge;"

For Maud soon thought the Judge a bore,
With all his learning and all his lore;

And the Judge would have bartered Maud's fair face
For more refinement and social grace.

If, of all words of tongue and pen,
The saddest are, "It might have been,"

More sad are these we daily see:
"It is, but hadn't ought to be."

A GEOLOGICAL MADRIGAL

I have found out a gift for my fair;
I know where the fossils abound,
Where the footprints of Aves declare
The birds that once walked on the ground.
Oh, come, and, in technical speech
We'll walk this Devonian shore,
Or on some Silurian beach
We'll wander, my love, evermore.

I will show thee the sinuous track
By the slow-moving Annelid made,
Or the Trilobite that, farther back,
In the old Potsdam sandstone was laid;
Thou shalt see, in his Jurassic tomb,
The Plesiosaurus embalmed;
In his Oolitic prime and his bloom,
Iguanodon safe and unharmed.

You wished, I remember it well,
And I loved you the more for that wish
For a perfect cystedian shell
And a WHOLE holocephalic fish.
And oh, if Earth's strata contains
In its lowest Silurian drift,
Or palaeozoic remains
The same, 'tis your lover's free gift!

Then come, love, and never say nay,
But calm all your maidenly fears;
We'll note, love, in one summer's day
The record of millions of years;
And though the Darwinian plan
Your sensitive feelings may shock,
We'll find the beginning of man,
Our fossil ancestors, in rock!

AVITOR

(AN AERIAL RETROSPECT)

What was it filled my youthful dreams,
In place of Greek or Latin themes,
Or beauty's wild, bewildering beams?
Avitor!

What visions and celestial scenes
I filled with aerial machines,
Montgolfier's and Mr. Green's!
Avitor!

What fairy tales seemed things of course!
The roc that brought Sindbad across,
The Calendar's own winged horse!
Avitor!

How many things I took for facts,
Icarus and his conduct lax,
And how he sealed his fate with wax!
Avitor!

The first balloons I sought to sail,
Soap-bubbles fair, but all too frail,
Or kites, but thereby hangs a tail.
Avitor!

What made me launch from attic tall
A kitten and a parasol,
And watch their bitter, frightful fall?
Avitor!

What youthful dreams of high renown
Bade me inflate the parson's gown,
That went not up, nor yet came down?
Avitor!

My first ascent I may not tell;
Enough to know that in that well
My first high aspirations fell.
Avitor!

My other failures let me pass:
The dire explosions, and, alas!
The friends I choked with noxious gas.
Avitor!

For lo! I see perfected rise
The vision of my boyish eyes,
The messenger of upper skies.
Avitor!

THE WILLOWS

(AFTER EDGAR ALLAN POE)

The skies they were ashen and sober,
The streets they were dirty and drear;
It was night in the month of October,
Of my most immemorial year.
Like the skies, I was perfectly sober,
As I stopped at the mansion of Shear,
At the Nightingale, perfectly sober,
And the willowy woodland down here.

Here, once in an alley Titanic
Of Ten-pins, I roamed with my soul,
Of Ten-pins, with Mary, my soul;
They were days when my heart was volcanic,
And impelled me to frequently roll,
And made me resistlessly roll,
Till my ten-strikes created a panic
In the realms of the Boreal pole,
Till my ten-strikes created a panic
With the monkey atop of his pole.

I repeat, I was perfectly sober,
But my thoughts they were palsied and sear,
My thoughts were decidedly queer;
For I knew not the month was October,
And I marked not the night of the year;
I forgot that sweet morceau of Auber
That the band oft performed down here,
And I mixed the sweet music of Auber
With the Nightingale's music by Shear.

And now as the night was senescent,
And star-dials pointed to morn,
And car-drivers hinted of morn,
At the end of the path a liquescent
And bibulous lustre was born;
'Twas made by the bar-keeper present,
Who mixed a duplicate horn,
His two hands describing a crescent
Distinct with a duplicate horn.

And I said: "This looks perfectly regal,
For it's warm, and I know I feel dry,
I am confident that I feel dry.
We have come past the emeu and eagle,
And watched the gay monkey on high;
Let us drink to the emeu and eagle,
To the swan and the monkey on high,
To the eagle and monkey on high;
For this bar-keeper will not inveigle,
Bully boy with the vitreous eye,

He surely would never inveigle,
Sweet youth with the crystalline eye."

But Mary, uplifting her finger,
Said: "Sadly this bar I mistrust,
I fear that this bar does not trust.
Oh, hasten! oh, let us not linger!
Oh, fly, let us fly, are we must!"
In terror she cried, letting sink her
Parasol till it trailed in the dust;
In agony sobbed, letting sink her
Parasol till it trailed in the dust,
Till it sorrowfully trailed in the dust.

Then I pacified Mary and kissed her,
And tempted her into the room,
And conquered her scruples and gloom;
And we passed to the end of the vista,
But were stopped by the warning of doom,
By some words that were warning of doom.
And I said, "What is written, sweet sister,
At the opposite end of the room?"
She sobbed, as she answered, "All liquors
Must be paid for ere leaving the room."

Then my heart it grew ashen and sober,
As the streets were deserted and drear,
For my pockets were empty and drear;
And I cried: "It was surely October,
On this very night of last year,
That I journeyed, I journeyed down here,
That I brought a fair maiden down here,
On this night of all nights in the year!
Ah! to me that inscription is clear;
Well I know now, I'm perfectly sober,
Why no longer they credit me here,
Well I know now that music of Auber,
And this Nightingale, kept by one Shear."

NORTH BEACH

(AFTER SPENSER)

Lo! where the castle of bold Pfeiffer throws
Its sullen shadow on the rolling tide,
No more the home where joy and wealth repose,
But now where wassailers in cells abide;
See yon long quay that stretches far and wide,
Well known to citizens as wharf of Meiggs:

There each sweet Sabbath walks in maiden pride
The pensive Margaret, and brave Pat, whose legs
Encased in broadcloth oft keep time with Peg's.

Here cometh oft the tender nursery-maid,
While in her ear her love his tale doth pour;
Meantime her infant doth her charge evade,
And rambleth sagely on the sandy shore,
Till the sly sea-crab, low in ambush laid,
Seizeth his leg and biteth him full sore.
Ah me! what sounds the shuddering echoes bore
When his small treble mixed with Ocean's roar!

Hard by there stands an ancient hostelrie,
And at its side a garden, where the bear,
The stealthy catamount, and coon agree
To work deceit on all who gather there;
And when Augusta, that unconscious fair
With nuts and apples plieth Bruin free,
Lo! the green parrot claweth her back hair,
And the gray monkey grabbeth fruits that she
On her gay bonnet wears, and laugheth loud in glee!

THE LOST TAILS OF MILETUS

High on the Thracian hills, half hid in the billows of clover,
Thyme, and the asphodel blooms, and lulled by Pactolian streamlet,
She of Miletus lay, and beside her an aged satyr
Scratched his ear with his hoof, and playfully mumbled his chestnuts.

Vainly the Maenid and the Bassarid gamboled about her,
The free-eyed Bacchante sang, and Pan, the renowned, the
Accomplished. Executed his difficult solo. In vain were their gambols and dances;
High o'er the Thracian hills rose the voice of the shepherdess, wailing:

"Ai! for the fleecy flocks, the meek-nosed, the passionless faces;
Ai! for the tallow-scented, the straight-tailed, the high-stepping;
Ai! for the timid glance, which is that which the rustic, sagacious,
Applies to him who loves but may not declare his passion!"

Her then Zeus answered slow: "O daughter of song and sorrow,
Hapless tender of sheep, arise from thy long lamentation!
Since thou canst not trust fate, nor behave as becomes a Greek maiden,
Look and behold thy sheep." And lo! they returned to her tailless!

THE RITUALIST

He wore, I think, a chasuble, the day when first we met;
A stole and snowy alb likewise, I recollect it yet.
He called me "daughter," as he raised his jeweled hand to bless;
And then, in thrilling undertones, he asked, "Would I confess?"

O mother dear! blame not your child, if then on bended knees
I dropped, and thought of Abelard, and also Eloise;
Or when, beside the altar high, he bowed before the pyx,
I envied that seraphic kiss he gave the crucifix.

The cruel world may think it wrong, perhaps may deem me weak,
And, speaking of that sainted man, may call his conduct "cheek;"
And, like that wicked barrister whom Cousin Harry quotes,
May term his mixed chalice "grog," his vestments "petticoats;"

But, whatsoe'er they do or say, I'll build a Christian's hope
On incense and on altar-lights, on chasuble and cope.
Let others prove, by precedent, the faith that they profess:
"His can't be wrong" that's symbolized by such becoming dress.

A MORAL VINDICATOR

If Mr. Jones, Lycurgus B.,
Had one peculiar quality,
'Twas his severe advocacy
Of conjugal fidelity.

His views of heaven were very free;
His views of life were painfully
Ridiculous; but fervently
He dwelt on marriage sanctity.

He frequently went on a spree;
But in his wildest revelry,
On this especial subject he
Betrayed no ambiguity.

And though at times Lycurgus B.
Did lay his hands not lovingly
Upon his wife, the sanctity
Of wedlock was his guaranty.

But Mrs. Jones declined to see
Affairs in the same light as he,
And quietly got a decree
Divorcing her from that L. B.

And what did Jones, Lycurgus B.,
With his known idiosyncrasy?
He smiled, a bitter smile to see,
And drew the weapon of Bowie.

He did what Sickles did to Key,
What Cole on Hiscock wrought, did he;
In fact, on persons twenty-three
He proved the marriage sanctity.

The counselor who took the fee,
The witnesses and referee,
The judge who granted the decree,
Died in that wholesale butchery.

And then when Jones, Lycurgus B.,
Had wiped the weapon of Bowie,
Twelve jurymen did instantly
Acquit and set Lycurgus free.

CALIFORNIA MADRIGAL

(ON THE APPROACH OF SPRING)

Oh, come, my beloved, from thy winter abode,
From thy home on the Yuba, thy ranch overflowed;
For the waters have fallen, the winter has fled,
And the river once more has returned to its bed.

Oh, mark how the spring in its beauty is near!
How the fences and tules once more reappear!
How soft lies the mud on the banks of yon slough
By the hole in the levee the waters broke through!

All nature, dear Chloris, is blooming to greet
The glance of your eye and the tread of your feet;
For the trails are all open, the roads are all free,
And the highwayman's whistle is heard on the lea.

Again swings the lash on the high mountain trail,
And the pipe of the packer is scenting the gale;
The oath and the jest ringing high o'er the plain,
Where the smut is not always confined to the grain.

Once more glares the sunlight on awning and roof,
Once more the red clay's pulverized by the hoof,
Once more the dust powders the "outsides" with red,
Once more at the station the whiskey is spread.

Then fly with me, love, ere the summer's begun,
And the mercury mounts to one hundred and one;
Ere the grass now so green shall be withered and sear,
In the spring that obtains but one month in the year.

WHAT THE ENGINES SAID

(OPENING OF THE PACIFIC RAILROAD)

What was it the Engines said,
Pilots touching, head to head
Facing on the single track,
Half a world behind each back?
This is what the Engines said,
Unreported and unread.

With a prefatory screech,
In a florid Western speech,
Said the Engine from the WEST:
"I am from Sierra's crest;
And if altitude's a test,
Why, I reckon, it's confessed
That I've done my level best."

Said the Engine from the EAST:
"They who work best talk the least.
S'pose you whistle down your brakes;
What you've done is no great shakes,
Pretty fair, but let our meeting
Be a different kind of greeting.
Let these folks with champagne stuffing,
Not their Engines, do the PUFFING.

"Listen! Where Atlantic beats
Shores of snow and summer heats;
Where the Indian autumn skies
Paint the woods with wampum dyes,
I have chased the flying sun,
Seeing all he looked upon,
Blessing all that he has blessed,
Nursing in my iron breast
All his vivifying heat,
All his clouds about my crest;
And before my flying feet
Every shadow must retreat."

Said the Western Engine, "Phew!"
And a long, low whistle blew.
"Come, now, really that's the oddest

Talk for one so very modest.
You brag of your East! YOU do?
Why, I bring the East to YOU!
All the Orient, all Cathay,
Find through me the shortest way;
And the sun you follow here
Rises in my hemisphere.
Really, if one must be rude,
Length, my friend, ain't longitude."

Said the Union: "Don't reflect, or
I'll run over some Director."
Said the Central: "I'm Pacific;
But, when riled, I'm quite terrific.
Yet to-day we shall not quarrel,
Just to show these folks this moral,
How two Engines in their vision
Once have met without collision."

That is what the Engines said,
Unreported and unread;
Spoken slightly through the nose,
With a whistle at the close.

THE LEGENDS OF THE RHINE

Beetling walls with ivy grown,
Frowning heights of mossy stone;
Turret, with its flaunting flag
Flung from battlemented crag;
Dungeon-keep and fortalice
Looking down a precipice
O'er the darkly glancing wave
By the Lurline-haunted cave;
Robber haunt and maiden bower,
Home of Love and Crime and Power,
That's the scenery, in fine,
Of the Legends of the Rhine.

One bold baron, double-dyed
Bigamist and parricide,
And, as most the stories run,
Partner of the Evil One;
Injured innocence in white,
Fair but idiotic quite,
Wringing of her lily hands;
Valor fresh from Paynim lands,
Abbot ruddy, hermit pale,
Minstrel fraught with many a tale,

Are the actors that combine
In the Legends of the Rhine.

Bell-mouthed flagons round a board;
Suits of armor, shield, and sword;
Kerchief with its bloody stain;
Ghosts of the untimely slain;
Thunder-clap and clanking chain;
Headsman's block and shining axe;
Thumb-screw, crucifixes, racks;
Midnight-tolling chapel bell,
Heard across the gloomy fell,
These and other pleasant facts
Are the properties that shine
In the Legends of the Rhine.

Maledictions, whispered vows
Underneath the linden boughs;
Murder, bigamy, and theft;
Travelers of goods bereft;
Rapine, pillage, arson, spoil,
Everything but honest toil,
Are the deeds that best define
Every Legend of the Rhine.

That Virtue always meets reward,
But quicker when it wears a sword;
That Providence has special care
Of gallant knight and lady fair;
That villains, as a thing of course,
Are always haunted by remorse,
Is the moral, I opine,
Of the Legends of the Rhine.

SONGS WITHOUT SENSE

FOR THE PARLOR AND PIANO

I. THE PERSONIFIED SENTIMENTAL

Affection's charm no longer gilds
The idol of the shrine;
But cold Oblivion seeks to fill
Regret's ambrosial wine.
Though Friendship's offering buried lies
'Neath cold Aversion's snow,
Regard and Faith will ever bloom
Perpetually below.

I see thee whirl in marble halls,
In Pleasure's giddy train;
Remorse is never on that brow,
Nor Sorrow's mark of pain.
Deceit has marked thee for her own;
Inconstancy the same;
And Ruin wildly sheds its gleam
Athwart thy path of shame.

II. THE HOMELY PATHETIC

The dews are heavy on my brow;
My breath comes hard and low;
Yet, mother dear, grant one request,
Before your boy must go.
Oh! lift me ere my spirit sinks,
And ere my senses fail,
Place me once more, O mother dear,
Astride the old fence-rail.

The old fence-rail, the old fence-rail!
How oft these youthful legs,
With Alice' and Ben Bolt's, were hung
Across those wooden pegs!
'Twas there the nauseating smoke
Of my first pipe arose:
O mother dear, these agonies
Are far less keen than those.

I know where lies the hazel dell,
Where simple Nellie sleeps;
I know the cot of Nettie Moore,
And where the willow weeps.
I know the brookside and the mill,
But all their pathos fails
Beside the days when once I sat
Astride the old fence-rails.

III. SWISS AIR

I'm a gay tra, la, la,
With my fal, lal, la, la,
And my bright
And my light
Tra, la, le.   [Repeat.]

Then laugh, ha, ha, ha,
And ring, ting, ling, ling,

And sing fal, la, la,
La, la, le.   [Repeat.]

VI. LITTLE POSTERITY

MASTER JOHNNY'S NEXT-DOOR NEIGHBOR

It was spring the first time that I saw her, for her papa and mamma
moved in
Next door, just as skating was over, and marbles about to begin;
For the fence in our back yard was broken, and I saw, as I peeped
through the slat,
There were "Johnny-jump-ups" all around her, and I knew it was
spring just by that.

I never knew whether she saw me, for she didn't say nothing to me,
But "Ma! here's a slat in the fence broke, and the boy that is next door can see."
But the next day I climbed on our wood-shed, as you know Mamma says I've a right,
And she calls out, "Well, peekin' is manners!" and I answered her, "Sass is perlite!"

But I wasn't a bit mad, no, Papa, and to prove it, the very next day,
When she ran past our fence in the morning I happened to get in her way,
For you know I am "chunked" and clumsy, as she says are all boys of my size,
And she nearly upset me, she did, Pa, and laughed till tears came in her eyes.

And then we were friends from that moment, for I knew that she told Kitty Sage,
And she wasn't a girl that would flatter "that she thought I was tall for my age."
And I gave her four apples that evening, and took her to ride on my sled,
And "What am I telling you this for?" Why, Papa, my neighbor is DEAD!

You don't hear one half I am saying, I really do think it's too bad!
Why, you might have seen crape on her door-knob, and noticed to-day I've been sad.
And they've got her a coffin of rosewood, and they say they have dressed her in white,
And I've never once looked through the fence, Pa, since she died—at eleven last night.

And Ma says it's decent and proper, as I was her neighbor and friend,
That I should go there to the funeral, and she thinks that YOU ought to attend;
But I am so clumsy and awkward, I know I shall be in the way,
And suppose they should speak to me, Papa, I wouldn't know just what to say.

So I think I will get up quite early, I know I sleep late, but I know
I'll be sure to wake up if our Bridget pulls the string that I'll tie to my toe;
And I'll crawl through the fence, and I'll gather the "Johnny-jump-ups" as they grew
Round her feet the first day that I saw her, and, Papa, I'll give them to you.

For you're a big man, and, you know, Pa, can come and go just where you choose,
And you'll take the flowers in to her, and surely they'll never refuse;
But, Papa, don't SAY they're from Johnny; THEY won't understand, don't you see?

But just lay them down on her bosom, and, Papa, SHE'LL know they're from Me.

MISS EDITH'S MODEST REQUEST

My Papa knows you, and he says you're a man who makes reading for books;
But I never read nothing you wrote, nor did Papa, I know by his looks.
So I guess you're like me when I talk, and I talk, and I talk all the day,
And they only say, "Do stop that child!" or, "Nurse, take Miss Edith away."

But Papa said if I was good I could ask you, alone by myself
If you wouldn't write me a book like that little one up on the shelf.
I don't mean the pictures, of course, for to make THEM you've got to be smart
But the reading that runs all around them, you know, just the easiest part.

You needn't mind what it's about, for no one will see it but me,
And Jane, that's my nurse, and John, he's the coachman, just only us three.
You're to write of a bad little girl, that was wicked and bold and all that;
And then you're to write, if you please, something good, very good, of a cat!

This cat, she was virtuous and meek, and kind to her parents, and mild,
And careful and neat in her ways, though her mistress was such a bad child;
And hours she would sit and would gaze when her mistress, that's me, was so bad,
And blink, just as if she would say, "Oh, Edith! you make my heart sad."

And yet, you would scarcely believe it, that beautiful, angelic cat
Was blamed by the servants for stealing whatever, they said, she'd get at.
And when John drank my milk, don't you tell me! I know just the way it was done,
They said 'twas the cat, and she sitting and washing her face in the sun!

And then there was Dick, my canary. When I left its cage open one day,
They all made believe that she ate it, though I know that the bird flew away.
And why? Just because she was playing with a feather she found on the floor.
As if cats couldn't play with a feather without people thinking 'twas more!

Why, once we were romping together, when I knocked down a vase from the shelf,
That cat was as grieved and distressed as if she had done it herself;
And she walked away sadly and hid herself, and never came out until tea,
So they say, for they sent ME to bed, and she never came even to me.

No matter whatever happened, it was laid at the door of that cat.
Why, once when I tore my apron, she was wrapped in it, and I called "Rat!"
Why, they blamed that on HER. I shall never, no, not to my dying day
Forget the pained look that she gave me when they slapped ME and took me away.

Of course, you know just what comes next, when a child is as lovely as that:
She wasted quite slowly away; it was goodness was killing that cat.
I know it was nothing she ate, for her taste was exceedingly nice;
But they said she stole Bobby's ice cream, and caught a bad cold from the ice.

And you'll promise to make me a book like that little one up on the shelf,
And you'll call her "Naomi," because it's a name that she just gave herself;
For she'd scratch at my door in the morning, and whenever I'd call out, "Who's there?"
She would answer, "Naomi! Naomi!" like a Christian, I vow and declare.

And you'll put me and her in a book. And mind, you're to say I was bad;
And I might have been badder than that but for the example I had.
And you'll say that she was a Maltese, and what's that you asked? "Is she dead?"
Why, please, sir, THERE AIN'T ANY CAT! You're to make one up out of your head!

MISS EDITH MAKES IT PLEASANT FOR BROTHER JACK

"Crying!" Of course I am crying, and I guess you would be crying, too,
If people were telling such stories as they tell about me, about YOU.
Oh yes, you can laugh if you want to, and smoke as you didn't care how,
And get your brains softened like uncle's. Dr. Jones says you're gettin' it now.

Why don't you say "Stop!" to Miss Ilsey? She cries twice as much as I do,
And she's older and cries just from meanness, for a ribbon or anything new.
Ma says it's her "sensitive nature." Oh my! No, I sha'n't stop my talk!
And I don't want no apples nor candy, and I don't want to go take a walk!

I know why you're mad! Yes, I do, now! You think that Miss Ilsey likes YOU,
And I've heard her REPEATEDLY call you the bold-facest boy that she knew;
And she'd "like to know where you learnt manners." Oh yes! Kick the table, that's right!
Spill the ink on my dress, and go then round telling Ma that I look like a fright!

What stories? Pretend you don't know that they're saying I broke off the match
Twixt old Money-grubber and Mary, by saying she called him "Crosspatch,"
When the only allusion I made him about sister Mary was, she
Cared more for his cash than his temper, and you know, Jack, you said that to me.

And it's true! But it's ME, and I'm scolded, and Pa says if I keep on I might
By and by get my name in the papers! Who cares? Why, 'twas only last night
I was reading how Pa and the sheriff were selling some lots, and it's plain
If it's awful to be in the papers, why, Papa would go and complain.

You think it ain't true about Ilsey? Well, I guess I know girls, and I say
There's nothing I see about Ilsey to show she likes you, anyway!
I know what it means when a girl who has called her cat after one boy
Goes and changes its name to another's. And she's done it and I wish you joy!

MISS EDITH MAKES ANOTHER FRIEND

Oh, you're the girl lives on the corner? Come in, if you want to, come quick!
There's no one but me in the house, and the cook but she's only a stick.
Don't try the front way, but come over the fence, through the window, that's how.

Don't mind the big dog, he won't bite you, just see him obey me! there, now!

What's your name? Mary Ellen? How funny! Mine's Edith, it's nicer, you see;
But yours does for you, for you're plainer, though maybe you're gooder than me;
For Jack says I'm sometimes a devil, but Jack, of all folks, needn't talk,
For I don't call the seamstress an angel till Ma says the poor thing must "walk."

Come in! It's quite dark in the parlor, for sister will keep the blinds down,
For you know her complexion is sallow like yours, but she isn't as brown;
Though Jack says that isn't the reason she likes to sit here with Jim Moore.
Do you think that he meant that she kissed him? Would you, if your lips wasn't sore?

If you like, you can try our piano. 'Tain't ours. A man left it here
To rent by the month, although Ma says he hasn't been paid for a year.
Sister plays, oh, such fine variations! why, I once heard a gentleman say
That she didn't mind THAT for the music in fact, it was just in her way!

Ain't I funny? And yet it's the queerest of all that, whatever I say,
One half of the folks die a-laughing, and the rest, they all look t'other way.
And some say, "That child!" Do they ever say that to such people as you?
Though maybe you're naturally silly, and that makes your eyes so askew.

Now stop, don't you dare to be crying! Just as sure as you live, if you do,
I'll call in my big dog to bite you, and I'll make my Papa kill you, too!
And then where'll you be? So play pretty. There's my doll, and a nice piece of cake.
You don't want it, you think it is poison! Then I'LL eat it, dear, just for your sake!

WHAT MISS EDITH SAW FROM HER WINDOW

Our window's not much, though it fronts on the street;
There's a fly in the pane that gets nothin' to eat;
But it's curious how people think it's a treat
For ME to look out of the window!

Why, when company comes, and they're all speaking low,
With their chairs drawn together, then some one says, "Oh!
Edith dear! that's a good child, now run, love, and go
And amuse yourself there at the window!"

Or Bob, that's my brother, comes in with his chum,
And they whisper and chuckle, the same words will come.
And it's "Edith, look here! Oh, I say! what a rum
Lot of things you can see from that window!"

And yet, as I told you, there's only that fly
Buzzing round in the pane, and a bit of blue sky,
And the girl in the opposite window, that I
Look at when SHE looks from HER window.

And yet, I've been thinking I'd so like to see
If what goes on behind HER, goes on behind ME!
And then, goodness gracious! what fun it would be
For us BOTH as we sit by our window!

How we'd know when the parcels were hid in a drawer,
Or things taken out that one never sees more;
What people come in and go out of the door,
That we never see from the window!

And that night when the stranger came home with our Jane
I might SEE what I HEARD then, that sounded so plain
Like when my wet fingers I rub on the pane
(Which they won't let ME do on my window).

And I'd know why papa shut the door with a slam,
And said something funny that sounded like "jam,"
And then "Edith, where are you?" I said, "Here I am."
"Ah, that's right, dear, look out of the window!"

They say when I'm grown up these things will appear
More plain than they do when I look at them here,
But I think I see some things uncommonly clear,
As I sit and look down from the window.

What things? Oh, the things that I make up, you know,
Out of stories I've read and they all pass below.
Ali Baba, the Forty Thieves, all in a row,
Go by, as I look from my window.

That's only at church time; other days there's no crowd.
Don't laugh! See that big man who looked up and bowed?
That's our butcher, I call him the Sultan Mahoud
When he nods to me here at the window!

And THAT man, he's our neighbor, just gone for a ride
Has three wives in the churchyard that lie side by side.
So I call him "Bluebeard" in search of his bride,
While I'm Sister Anne at the window.

And what do I call you? Well, here's what I DO:
When my sister expects you, she puts me here, too;
But I wait till you enter, to see if it's you,
And then, I just OPEN the window!

"Dear child!" Yes, that's me! "Oh, you ask what that's for?
Well, Papa says you're 'Poverty's self,' and what's more,
I open the window, when YOU'RE at the door,
To see Love fly out of the window!"

ON THE LANDING

(AN IDYL OF THE BALUSTERS)

BOBBY, aetat. 3 1/2. JOHNNY, aetat. 4 1/2.

BOBBY
Do you know why they've put us in that back room,
Up in the attic, close against the sky,
And made believe our nursery's a cloak-room?
Do you know why?

JOHNNY
No more I don't, nor why that Sammy's mother,
What Ma thinks horrid, 'cause he bunged my eye,
Eats an ice cream, down there, like any other!
No more don't I!

BOBBY
Do you know why Nurse says it isn't manners
For you and me to ask folks twice for pie,
And no one hits that man with two bananas?
Do you know why?

JOHNNY
No more I don't, nor why that girl, whose dress is
Off of her shoulders, don't catch cold and die,
When you and me gets croup when WE undresses!
No more don't I!

BOBBY
Perhaps she ain't as good as you and I is,
And God don't want her up there in the sky,
And lets her live, to come in just when pie is
Perhaps that's why!

JOHNNY
Do you know why that man that's got a cropped head
Rubbed it just now as if he felt a fly?
Could it be, Bobby, something that I dropped?
And is that why?

BOBBY
Good boys behaves, and so they don't get scolded,
Nor drop hot milk on folks as they pass by.

JOHNNY (piously)
Marbles would bounce on Mr. Jones' bald head

But I sha'n't try!

BOBBY
Do you know why Aunt Jane is always snarling
At you and me because we tells a lie,
And she don't slap that man that called her darling?
Do you know why?

JOHNNY
No more I don't, nor why that man with Mamma
Just kissed her hand.

BOBBY
She hurt it and that's why;
He made it well, the very way that Mamma
Does do to I.

JOHNNY
I feel so sleepy.... Was that Papa kissed us?
What made him sigh, and look up to the sky?

BOBBY
We weren't downstairs, and he and God had missed us,
And that was why!

NOTES

1 - THE LOST GALLEON. As the custom on which the central incident of this legend is based may not be familiar to all readers, I will repeat here that it is the habit of navigators to drop a day from their calendar in crossing westerly the 180th degree of longitude of Greenwich, adding a day in coming east; and that the idea of the lost galleon had an origin as prosaic as the log of the first China Mail Steamer from San Francisco. The explanation of the custom and its astronomical relations belongs rather to the usual text-books than to poetical narration. If any reader thinks I have overdrawn the credulous superstitions of the ancient navigators, I refer him to the veracious statements of Maldonado, De Fonte, the later voyages of La Perouse and Anson, and the charts of 1640. In the charts of that day Spanish navigators reckoned longitude E. 360 degrees from the meridian of the Isle of Ferro. For the sake of perspicuity before a modern audience, the more recent meridian of Madrid was substituted. The custom of dropping a day at some arbitrary point in crossing the Pacific westerly, I need not say, remains unaffected by any change of meridian. I know not if any galleon was ever really missing. For two hundred and fifty years an annual trip was made between Acapulco and Manila. It may be some satisfaction to the more severely practical of my readers to know that, according to the best statistics of insurance, the loss during that period would be exactly three vessels and six hundredths of a vessel, which would certainly justify me in this summary disposition of ONE.

2 - THE PLIOCENE SKULL. This extraordinary fossil is in the possession of Prof. Josiah D. Whitney, of the State Geological Survey of California. The poem was based on the following paragraph from the daily press of 1868: "A human skull has been found in California, in the pliocene formation. This skull is the remnant not only of the earliest pioneer of this State, but the oldest known human being....The skull was found in a shaft 150 feet deep, two miles from Angels in Calaveras County, by a miner named James Watson, who gave it to Mr. Scribner, a merchant, who gave it to Dr. Jones, who sent it to the State Geological Survey.... The published volume of the State Survey of the Geology of California states that man existed here contemporaneously with the mastodon, but this fossil proves that he was here before the mastodon was known to exist."

A Short Biography of Bret Harte

American writer and poet Bret Harte was born Francis Brett Harte in Albany, New York in 1836. Throughout his life, Harte also worked as a teacher, a miner, a journalist and an American diplomat in Europe. He is best remembered today for his iconic short stories, poems and articles about the California Gold Rush of the mid-19th century.

Although his formal education was sporadic and ended for good when he was only thirteen, Harte read and wrote from a young age. The earliest record of his published work cites a satirical poem called *Autumn Musings,* written when he was just eleven years old and published in the New York *Sunday Atlas.* After the death of his schoolteacher father in 1853, Harte's family moved to Oakland, California where his mother had remarried (to Col. Andrew Williams, a future mayor of Oakland). Harte took up a series of diverse occupations before settling into a life-long career in letters.

Following several years of teaching and working as a miner further along the coast in Humboldt's Bay, Harte became an editor and journalist with the weekly newspaper *Northern Californian*. After writing an editorial condemnation of the infamous 1860 massacre of a local community of Wiyot Native Americans by white settlers and vigilante militia, Harte's life was threatened and he was forced to re-locate back to the San Francisco area. Here he continued to write, publishing his first poetry and prose pieces in *The Californian* and *The Golden Era*, both newly established literary journals. During the Civil War (1861-1865) Harte identified as an Abolitionist and wrote patriotic propaganda poetry.

Harte married Anna Griswold, with whom he went on to have four children, on August 11, 1862, in San Rafael, California. By all accounts the marriage was at times somewhat difficult. Now a family man, Harte supplemented his still meager earnings from writing and editing by briefly taking a job with the United States Mint. It was also around this time that he started using the pen name Bret Harte. He published a collection of poems called *The Lost Galleon and Other Tales* under this name in 1867.

In 1868, Harte became founding editor at *The Overland Monthly*, a literary journal that would publish Harte's *The Luck of Roaring Camp* later that same year. The short story about an orphan child raised by prospectors made Harte's reputation in North America and remains one of his best-loved works. The story is considered classic Harte with its exploration of physical hardship within an unforgiving landscape and the possibility of redemption for the colourful hardscrabble inhabitants who moved through it.

Other important Harte works published in *Overland Monthly* during Harte's tenure there include *Dickens in Camp,* a tribute to Charles Dickens upon the death of the great author in 1870 and the narrative poem *Plain Language from Truthful James* (also known as *The Heathen Chinee*). Harte intended the latter as a satirical jab against anti-Chinese prejudice within the white working class. However, it was more popularly received as a mocking portrayal of Chinese Californians, then performing many of the most menial jobs in the mining camps and frontier towns of the West Coast. Harte later distanced himself from the work, calling it "the worst poem I ever wrote, possibly the worst poem anyone ever wrote."

Also while at *Overland Monthly*, Harte famously commissioned work from a fledgling writer named Samuel Clemons with whom he would collaborate almost a decade later. Though younger than Clemons, Harte became established as a writer first and for a time he was a mentor to the man who would become Mark Twain, reading and critiquing early manuscripts.

By the time Harte left the journal in 1870, he was both well known and well paid, a star of the American literary scene. It's not difficult to understand why. Harte's emphasis on the rollicking and the rough and ready in his stories, poems and "sketches" set in the West during the California Gold Rush was in sharp contrast to the staid Victorian sentimentality of the prevailing literature of the day. Harte's prose style was energetic and raw by comparison, his work peopled with grotesque and fantastic characters; it reflected American history and experience in a welcome and unique way.

So much so that *The Atlantic Monthly* magazine wooed Hart back East with the unprecedented offer of $10,000 to write a monthly story or poem for them for a year. In many ways, the contract was the pinnacle of Harte's career and it ushered in a period of declining fortune for the writer. He wrote two novels – *M'Liss* in 1873 and *Gabriel Conroy* in 1876 – both flopped. His contract with *The Atlantic Monthly* went un-renewed and Harte was once again forced to lecture, write advertising copy and otherwise freelance to survive.

In 1877 Harte also embarked on several more ill fated creative ventures. One of them was a play based on the character of Ah Sin, hero of the poem *Plain Language from Truthful James*. He co-wrote the play with Twain, who by then was becoming very well known as a writer and humourist, and it opened on Broadway – but it was not successful. The friends quarreled and parted company for good. Twain later had harsh words for Harte, writing critically in his autobiography that Harte was "insincere" and not to be trusted in personal matters. He referred to Harte as "The Immortal Bilk". The failed collaboration and Twain's vocal harshness about whose fault it was further tarnished Harte's reputation and the writer found his remaining opportunities drying up.

Harte left America in 1878 and was never to return. Thanks to some powerfully connected friends, he asked for and received postings as a United States Consul, first in Germany, then in Scotland.

Rather than moving back home to Boston where his family had remained, Harte moved to London, England following his consular tours of duty. He spent his final years in that city, writing prolifically but without real acclaim. Nonetheless, Harte did write some influential works while living in Europe, notably the short story, *The Outcasts of Poker Flat*. The tale follows the fortunes of four miscreant outcasts from the California gold camp of Poker Flat and features the eccentric characters and regional colour that originally made Harte famous. Not so surprisingly, the story has been reworked for different disciplines. An opera version by American composer Stanworth Beckler was performed in 1960 at the College of the Pacific in Stockton, California; another version by composer Samuel Adler appeared in 1962. The story also spawned multiple film versions – one with screen stars Preston Foster, Margaret Irving and Van Heflin in 1937 and one with Dale Robertson (best know as the host of the television series Death Valley Days) in 1952, among others. Harte's story *Tennessee's Partner* was also made into a movie starring John Payne and Ronald Reagan in 1955.

Up to the very end, Harte mined the scenarios and themes of California, the West and the Gold Rush era, with the short story collections Under the Redwoods (1901) and *Opening in the Old Trail* (1902) being his final works. In his later writing years, he remained marginally more popular in Europe and the UK than in his homeland, where literary tastes had moved on.

On May 5th, 1902, Harte died of throat cancer at the age of 65. At that time, he was living in Camberley, Surrey on the estate of the wealthy Van de Velde family who had been supporting him for some years. He is buried in the village churchyard in nearby Frimley. Inscribed on his gravestone are the words "Death shall reap the braver harvest".

Today, Harte is still considered an important figure in the evolution of a distinct and independent American literary style. He was one of the first to write from personal knowledge about the frontier experience in California and the West, originating many of the archetypes and stock characters – the rugged miners, desperate gamblers, schoolmarms and prostitutes with hearts of gold – that we still associate with the Western genre in literature and popular culture to this day. His successful *Condensed Novels,* in which he wrote in the style of many established literary figures of the day, reveal the mix and breadth of his talents as well as his confidence. Equally his taste for writing in dialect can at times seem exhibitionist and was another issue that Twain remarked negatively on.

Though more than one literary critic has suggested that Harte's oeuvre failed to evolve past his initial successes and that he repeated a limited number of essential plotlines, themes and characterizations with each new work created, his contributions to American literary history are still regularly re-assessed and re-considered by contemporary academics. Reviews of his work and their value continue to be very mixed, yet Harte and his place in American literary history have not been forgotten.

Bret Harte – A Concise Bibliography

The Lost Galleon and Other Tales (1867)
Condensed Novels (1867)
The Luck of Roaring Camp (1870)
Plain Language from Truthful James (1870)
Poems (1871)
East and West Poems (1871)
Stories of the Sierras and Other Sketches (1872)
The Little Drummer (1872)
Mrs. Skaggs' Husbands (1873)
M'Liss (1873)
Tales of the Argonauts (1875)
Echoes of the Foot-Hills (1875)
Wan Lee: The Pagan (1876)
Two Men of Sandy Bar (1876)
Gabriel Conroy (1876)
Thankful Blossom (1877)
The Story of a Mine (1878)
Drift from Two Shores (1878)
The Twins of Table Mountain (1879)
Poetical Works (1880)
Flip and Found at Blazing Star (1882)
In the Carquinez Woods (1883)
On the Frontier (1884)

By Shore and Sedge (1885)
Maruja (1885)
The Queen of the Pirate Isle (1886)
Snow-Bound at Eagle's (1886)
The Crusade of the Excelsior (1887)
A Millionaire of Rough-and-Ready (1887)
A Phyllis of the Sierras (1888)
The Argonauts of North Liberty (1888)
Cressy (1889)
The Heritage of Dedlow Marsh (1889)
A Ward of the Golden Gate (1890)
A Waif of the Plains (1890)
A Sappho of the Green Springs (1891)
A First Family of Tasajara (1891)
Colonel Starbottle's Client (1892)
Susy: A Story of the Plains (1893)
Sally Dows (1893)
A Protégée of Jack Hamlin's (1894)
The Bell-Ringer of Angel's (1894)
Clarence (1895)
In a Hollow of the Hills (1895)
Poetical Works of Bret Harte (1896)
Barker's Luck and Other Stories (1896)
Three Partners (1897)
Some Later Verses (1898)
Tales of Trail and Town (1898)
Stories in Light and Shadow (1898)
Mr. Jack Hamlin's Meditation (1899)
The Complete Poetical Works (1899)
From Sand Hill to Pine (1900)
Under the Redwoods (1901)
Condensed Novels: Second Series (1902)
Sue: A Play in Three Acts (1902)
Openings in the Old Trail (1902)
Trent's Trust (1903)
The Lectures of Bret Harte (1909)
Poems and Stories (1912)
The Works of Bret Harte (1914)
The Story of Enriquez (1924)
Sketches of the Sixties (1926)
The Letters of Bret Harte (1926)